All-Star

1

Linda Lee

Stephen Sloan ★ Grace Tanaka ★ Shirley Velasco

McGraw-Hill ESL/ELT

All-Star 1 First Edition

Published by McGraw-Hill ESL/ELT, a business unit of The McGraw-Hill Companies, Inc. 1221 Avenue of the Americas, New York, NY 10020. Copyright © 2005 by The McGraw-Hill Companies, Inc. All rights reserved. No part of this publication may be reproduced or distributed in any form or by any means, or stored in a database or retrieval system, without the prior written consent of The McGraw-Hill Companies, Inc., including, but not limited to, in any network or other electronic storage or transmission, or broadcast for distance learning.

3 4 5 6 7 8 9 10   WCT   09 08 07 06 05 04

ISBN 0-07-284664-X (Student Book)
ISBN 0-07-304871-2 (Student Book with Audio Highlights)
ISBN 0-07-111488-2 (Student Book – International Student Edition)

Editorial director Tina B. Carver
Executive editor Erik Gundersen
Director of sales and marketing Thomas P. Dare
Developmental editors Jennifer Monaghan, Mari Vargo
Editorial assistant David Averbach
Production manager Juanita Thompson
Interior designer Wee Design Group
Cover designer Wee Design Group
Illustrators Gioia Fiommenghi, Andrew Lange, Chris Pappas, Carlos Sanchis/NETS, Blanche Sims, Susan Tait-Porcaro, Chris Winn, David Winter, and Jerry Zimmerman
Photo Research NETS
Photo Credits

14 *(left to right, row one)* © Getty Images, © Jonathan Nourok/PhotoEdit, © Dana White/PhotoEdit; (row two) © Michael Newman/PhotoEdit, © Phil Martin/PhotoEdit, © Spencer Grant/PhotoEdit; *(row three)* © Tom Prettyman/PhotoEdit, © Billy E. Barnes/PhotoEdit, © David Young-Wolff/PhotoEdit

30 © Bill Aron/PhotoEdit

31 *(left to right)* © Michelle D. Bridwell/PhotoEdit, © Dennis MacDonald/PhotoEdit

58 *(top to bottom)* © Jeff Greenberg/PhotoEdit, © Mark Richards/PhotoEdit

59 *(clockwise from upper left)* © Bill Aron/PhotoEdit, © Getty Images, © Getty Images, © A. Ramey/PhotoEdit

78 *(left to right, all)* © Getty Images

79 *(table, left to right, row 1, all)* © Getty Images; (row 2, all) © Getty Images; (bottom, left to right) © Getty Images, © David Young-Wolff/PhotoEdit, © Getty Images

106 © Getty Images

107 *(clockwise from top left)* © Lina Sokolson, © Getty Images, © Spencer Grant/PhotoEdit

110 *(top right)* © Getty Images; *(table, row 1, left to right)* © Cleve Bryant/PhotoEdit, © Getty Images, © Getty Images, © Getty Images *(row 2)* © David Young-Wolff/PhotoEdit, © Getty Images, Getty Images, © Getty Images; *(row three)* © Lon C. Diehl/PhotoEdit, © Bill Aron/PhotoEdit, © Stephen McBrady/PhotoEdit

126 *(top left)* © Tony Freeman; *(top right)* © Michael Newman/PhotoEdit; *(bottom left)* © Michael Newman/PhotoEdit; *(bottom right)* © Spencer Grant/PhotoEdit

139 *(left to right)* © Patrick O'Lear/PhotoEdit, © Jeff Greenberg/PhotoEdit, © Jeff Greenberg/PhotoEdit

142 © Getty Images

145 © Getty Images

158 © Getty Images

ACKNOWLEDGEMENTS

The authors and publisher would like to thank the following individuals who reviewed the *All-Star* program at various stages of development and whose comments, reviews, and field-testing were instrumental in helping us shape the series:

Carol Antunano • The English Center; Miami, FL

Feliciano Atienza • YMCA Elesair Project; New York, NY

Nancy Baxer • Lutheran Social Ministries of New Jersey Refugee Resettlement Program; Trenton, NJ

Jeffrey P. Bright • Albany Park Community Center; Chicago, IL

Enzo Caserta • Miami Palmetto Adult Education Center; Miami, FL

Allison Freiman • YMCA Elesair Project; New York, NY

Susan Gaer • Santa Ana College School of Continuing Education; Santa Ana, CA

Toni Galaviz • Reseda Community Adult School; Reseda, CA

Maria Hegarty • SCALE; Somerville, MA

Virginia Hernandez • Miami Palmetto Adult Education Center; Miami, FL

Giang Hoang • Evans Community Adult School; Los Angeles, CA

Edwina Hoffman • Miami-Dade County Adult Schools; Miami, FL

Ionela Istrate • YMCA of Greater Boston International Learning Center; Boston, MA

Janice Jensen • Santa Ana College School of Continuing Education; Santa Ana, CA

Jan Jerrell • San Diego Community College District; San Diego, CA

Margaret Kirkpatrick • Berkeley Adult School; Berkeley, CA

LaRanda Marr • Oakland Unified School District; Office of Adult Education; Oakland, CA

Patricia Mooney-Gonzalez • New York State Department of Education; Albany, NY

Paula Orias • Piper Community School; Broward County Public Schools; Sunrise, FL

Linda O'Roke • City College of San Francisco; San Francisco, CA

Betsy Parrish • Hamline University; St. Paul, MN

Mary Pierce • Xavier Adult School; New York, NY

Marta Pitt • Lindsey Hopkins Technical Education Center; Miami, FL

Donna Price-Machado • San Diego Community College District; San Diego, CA

Sylvia Ramirez • Community Learning Center • MiraCosta College; Oceanside, CA

Inna Reydel • YMCA of Greater Boston International Learning Center; Boston, MA

Kristin Sherman • Adult ESL Program; Central Piedmont Community College; Charlotte, NC

Leslie Shimazaki • San Diego Community College District; San Diego, CA

Betty Stone • SCALE; Somerville, MA

Theresa Suslov • SCALE; Somerville, MA

Dave VanLew • Simi Valley Adult & Career Institute; Simi Valley, CA

Scope and Sequence

UNIT	Life Skills				
	Listening and Speaking	Reading and Writing	Critical Thinking	Vocabulary	Grammar
Pre-Unit **Meeting Your Classmates** *page 2*	• Listen to introductions • Introduce yourself • Ask for and give spelling of names	• Make a name tag		• Personal information (first name, last name) • Alphabet	
1 **Getting Started** *page 4*	• Exchange personal information • Talk about things in a classroom • Follow classroom instructions • Say and understand numbers (telephone, area code, zip code) • Use appropriate greetings and partings • Ask about occupations • Introduce people **Pronunciation Focus:** Long vowel sounds: *I* and *E*	• Read a world map • Read and write classroom instructions • Read for specific information • Read job ads • Read and complete application forms • Make flashcards	• Classify information • Apply what you know • Interpret information (on an application form) • Interpret a world map	• Classroom vocabulary • Countries • Personal information (name, address, etc.) • Occupations	• Personal pronouns • Imperatives • Punctuation **Spotlight:** Simple present of *be*; possessives
2 **Places** *page 20*	• Describe the location of things in the community • Talk about places on a U.S. map • Ask for clarification • Talk about library services **Pronunciation Focus:** Voiced and voiceless *Th* sounds	• Use a telephone directory • Read a map • Read traffic signs • Complete an application for a library card • Write addresses and phone numbers **Spotlight:** Personal interest stories	• Interpret a map • Classify places (public/private) • Interpret an illustration • Interpret traffic signs	• Geographical directions (N, S, E, W) • Places in the community • People and things in a library • Street signs	• Prepositions of location • *There is/There are* • *Is there/Are there* • Singular and plural nouns • Punctuation
3 **Time and Money** *page 36*	• Ask for and tell the time of day • Ask about business hours • Ask about prices • Ask for a phone number from directory assistance • Listen to an automated phone message **Pronunciation Focus:** Syllable stress in numbers	• Read amounts of money • Read and write personal checks • Read a time schedule • Read signs (in the library) • Write time schedules • Describe a scene • Write amounts of money in words and numbers	• Draw conclusions • Classify information • Compare	• Times of day • Time words • Days of the week • Money: coins and bills • Parts of a personal check	• *Yes/no* questions with *be* • Questions with *how much* **Spotlight:** *Yes/No* questions and answers with *be*; information questions with *be*

Correlations to National Standards

Civics Concepts	Math Skills	CASAS Life Skill Competencies	SCANS Competencies (Workplace)	EFF Content Standards	Literacy Completion Points (LCPs)
		• 0.1.4, 0.1.6, 0.2.1	• Sociability	• Communicate so that others understand	• 22.02
• Identify countries on a map • Recognize different occupations in the community	• Use numbers 0 to 11 • Understand page references • Read and write telephone numbers and addresses	• **1:** 0.1.2, 0.2.1, 1.1.3, 2.7.2, 6.6.5 • **2:** 0.1.5, 2.2.1, 6.6.5, 7.1.4, 7.4.1 • **3:** 0.1.5, 6.0.2, 7.1.3 • **4:** 0.2.2 • **5:** 0.1.4, 0.1.1 • **6:** 4.1.3, 4.1.8, 4.6.3 • **7:** 0.1.2, 7.1.4, 7.4.7, 7.4.8 • **GS:** 0.1.6	Emphasized are the following: • Know how to learn • See things in the mind's eye • Sociability • Work well with others • Work with people of diverse backgrounds	Emphasized are the following: • Communicate so that others understand • Listen to and learn from others' experiences and ideas	• **1:** 30.02, 32.07, 33.09 • **2:** 33.02 • **3:** 25.01, 32.07 • **4:** 22.01, 32.04, 33.07 • **5:** 22.02, 22.03, 33.02 • **6:** 18.01 • **7:** 32.13 • **GS:** 22.01, 32.02, 33.03
• Identify public services • Locate cities and states in the U.S. • Make a neighborhood map • Identify places in the community • Understand traffic signs • Visit a public library • Complete a library card application	• Understand phone numbers • Read math symbols • Understand spatial relationships	• **1:** 0.1.2, 2.1.1, 2.2.5, 6.7.3 • **2:** 0.1.2, 0.1.6, 1.1.3, 1.9.4 • **3:** 0.1.2, 2.2.1, 2.2.3 • **4:** 1.9.4, 2.2.2, 5.2.4, 6.0.3, 6.0.4 • **5:** 0.1.2, 0.1.6, 2.5.4, 2.6.1 • **6:** 0.1.2, 2.5.5, 2.5.6 • **7:** 0.1.2, 7.1.4, 7.4.7, 7.4.8 • **WS:** 0.2.4, 4.6.1, 7.5.1	Emphasized are the following: • See things in the mind's eye • Understand how systems work	Emphasized are the following: • Get involved in the community and get others involved • Assist others • Find and use community resources and services	• **1:** 29.01 • **2:** 29.01, 32.01, 32.10 • **3:** 26.04, 32.02 • **4:** 26.03, 32.01, 32.06 • **5:** 26.03, 32.01, 32.02 • **6:** 29.01 • **7:** 32.08, 32.13 • **WS:** 32.10, 33.01
• Identify the business hours of places in the community • Distinguish U.S. coins and bills	• Interpret clock time • Use numbers 12 to 90 • Write the time using numbers • Count coins and bills • Read and understand price tags • Write dollar amounts on personal checks • Use addition and subtraction to calculate total costs	• **1:** 0.1.2, 2.3.1, 6.0.2 • **2:** 0.1.2, 0.1.6, 2.3.2, 2.5.4 • **3:** 1.1.2, 1.1.6, 6.0.1 • **4:** 1.8.2, 6.1.1, 6.5.1, 7.3.2 • **5:** 0.1.3, 0.1.4, 2.1.8 • **6:** 1.2.1, 1.2.2, 2.1.1 • **7:** 0.1.2, 7.1.4, 7.4.7, 7.4.8 • **GS:** 7.2.3	Emphasized are the following: • Understand how systems work	Emphasized are the following: • Manage time and resources • Learn new skills	• **1:** 25.01, 25.02 • **2:** 25.03 • **3:** 25.05 • **4:** 32.08 • **5:** 23.02, 25.04 • **6:** 32.07 • **7:** 32.13, 34.02 • **GS:** 33.02, 33.06, 33.07

CASAS and LCP standards: Numbers in bold indicate lesson numbers. • **GS**: Grammar Spotlight • **WS**: Writing Spotlight

Scope and Sequence

Correlations to National Standards

Civics Concepts	Math Skills	CASAS Life Skill Competencies	SCANS Competencies (Workplace)	EFF Content Standards	Literacy Completion Points (LCPs)
• Identify important holidays in the U.S. • Keep community appointments on a calendar • Interpret a child's school calendar	• Use ordinal numbers • Read and write dates • Convert dates to numeric form • Interpret schedules • Understand appointment times and dates	• **1:** 0.1.2, 2.3.2, 6.0.2, 2.7.1 • **2:** 0.1.4, 0.2.3, 2.6.3, 2.7.3 • **3:** 6.0.1, 7.1.2 • **4:** 0.1.2, 2.7.1, 2.7.2 • **5:** 0.1.4, 2.1.8, 3.1.2 • **6:** 2.3.2, 7.1.1, 7.1.4 • **7:** 0.1.2, 7.1.4, 7.4.7, 7.4.8 • **WS:** 2.7.1, 7.5.1	Emphasized are the following: • Problem solving • Self-management • Acquire and evaluate information • Organize and maintain information	Emphasized are the following: • Manage time and resources • Pass on values, ethics, and cultural heritage • Organize, plan, and prioritize work	• **1:** 25.03, 29.03, 30.01 • **2:** 25.01, 32.01, 32.07 • **3:** 24.03, 25.04, 32.02 • **4:** 32.07, 32.10 • **5:** 24.03, 34.03 • **6:** 31.04 • **7:** 32.04, 32.13 • **WS:** 33.06
• Explore a department store • Interpret price tags and receipts • Recognize different occupations in the community	• Understand prices and sales receipts • Use multiplication and division to calculate totals	• **1:** 1.1.9, 1.3.9, 6.6.5 • **2:** 1.3.1, 1.3.7 • **3:** 1.1.4, 1.2.1, 1.2.2, 1.2.4, 4.4.1, 6.1.3 • **4:** 7.2.7 • **5:** 8.1.2 • **6:** 4.4.1, 8.4.1 • **7:** 0.1.2, 7.1.4, 7.4.7, 7.4.8 • **GS:** 7.4.3	Emphasized are the following: • Creative thinking • Reasoning • See things in the mind's eye • Analyze and communicate information	Emphasized are the following: • Provide for physical needs • Reflect on and reevaluate opinions and ideas	• **1:** 28.02 • **2:** 33.03 • **3:** 28.03, 33.03 • **4:** 22.03 • **5:** 19.01 • **6:** 19.01 • **7:** 32.08, 32.10, 32.13 • **GS:** 33.02
• Understand the food groups • Explore a grocery store • Interpret receipts • Understand healthy eating	• Use U.S. measurements: pounds, ounces, and cups • Compare prices • Budget for food • Calculate serving sizes • Read and write measurements for recipes	• **1:** 1.3.8 • **2:** 0.1.2, 1.3.8 • **3:** 1.1.4, 1.1.7, 1.3.8, 6.5.1 • **4:** 1.2.2, 1.2.4, 1.2.5 • **5:** 1.3.3 • **6:** 3.5.1, 3.5.2, 3.5.9 • **7:** 0.1.2, 7.1.4, 7.4.7, 7.4.8 • **WS:** 1.1.1, 8.2.1	Emphasized are the following: • Decision making • Problem solving • See things in the mind's eye • Self-management • Use resources wisely • Teach others new skills • Acquire and evaluate information	Emphasized are the following: • Find and use community resources and services • Find, interpret, and analyze diverse sources of information • Provide for physical needs • Communicate so that others understand	• **1:** 24.05 • **2:** 32.01 • **3:** 28.01 • **4:** 25.05, 28.03 • **5:** 32.01 • **6:** 32.04, 32.07 • **7:** 32.08, 32.13 • **WS:** 32.07
• Discuss community-related activities	• Take messages that include telephone numbers • Create a household budget • Use addition and multiplication to calculate totals	• **1:** 0.2.1, 6.6.8 • **2:** 8.2.1, 8.2.5, 8.2.6, 8.3.1 • **3:** 0.2.4, 2.7.2 • **4:** 7.5.1 • **5:** 2.1.7, 2.1.8 • **6:** 1.5.1, 7.4.9, 7.5.5, 7.5.7 • **7:** 0.1.2, 7.1.4, 7.4.7, 7.4.8 • **GS:** 7.2.2, 7.2.5, 7.3.3	Emphasized are the following: • Self-management • Integrity and honesty • Use resources wisely • Acquire and evaluate information • Organize and maintain information	Emphasized are the following: • Provide a nurturing home environment • Provide for physical needs • Teach children • Establish rules and expectations for children's behavior	• **1:** 31.01 • **2:** 31.03 • **3:** 34.02 • **4:** 34.03 • **5:** 32.02 • **6:** 32.08 • **7:** 32.02, 32.13 • **GS:** 33.07

CASAS and LCP standards: Numbers in bold indicate lesson numbers.   •   **GS**: Grammar Spotlight   •   **WS**: Writing Spotlight

Scope and Sequence

	Life Skills				
UNIT	Listening and Speaking	Reading and Writing	Critical Thinking	Vocabulary	Grammar
8 **Health** *page 116*	• Talk about health problems • Discuss remedies • Listen to and practice 911 calls **Pronunciation Focus:** Linking vowel to vowel with a *Y* or *W* sound	• Read warning labels • Read opinion paragraphs • Read bar graphs • Indent a paragraph • Write an opinion paragraph • Draw a bar graph **Spotlight:** Opinions	• Classify information • Make inferences • Analyze arguments • Make decisions	• Parts of the body • Health problems • Remedies • Safety warnings	• *Can* for ability • Giving advice with *should* and *shouldn't*
9 **House and Home** *page 132*	• Describe things in a house • Talk about accidents in the home • Ask for housing information **Pronunciation Focus:** Stress in compound nouns	• Write a comparison of two houses • Read bar graphs • Read classified ads • Write a classified ad • Read bills • Write personal checks	• Compare and contrast • Choose the best alternative • Classify information • Make decisions	• Areas of a house • Household furniture and other items • Features of a house • Types of housing • Classified ad abbreviations • Utility bills	• Comparing past and present • Simple past statements • Negative simple past statements **Spotlight:** Simple past statements; information questions with the simple past
10 **Work** *page 148*	• Respond to job ads • Listen to a job interview • Give opinions about what to do in an interview • Give reasons **Pronunciation Focus:** Stressing important words in sentences	• Read and write help wanted ads • Read a success story • Write a story • Read for specific information • Complete job applications • Complete an idea list **Spotlight:** Past tense stories	• Classify information • Reason • Sequence events	• Occupations and skills • Help wanted ad abbreviations • Work experience	• *Yes/No* questions with the simple past • Future with *be going to*

Correlations to National Standards

Civics Concepts	Math Skills	CASAS Life Skill Competencies	SCANS Competencies (Workplace)	EFF Content Standards	Literacy Completion Points (LCPs)
• Explore a health clinic • Understand safety warnings • Understand when to call 911 • Explore a hospital	• Use U.S. measurements: gallons, quarts, pints, cups and ounces • Interpret bar graphs	• **1**: 3.1.1 • **2**: 3.1.1 • **3**: 3.4.3 • **4**: 3.3.1, 3.4.1, 3.4.2, 6.6.1 • **5**: 2.1.2, 2.5.1 • **6**: 2.2.1, 3.1.3, 2.5.3, 7.4.4 • **7**: 0.1.2, 7.1.4, 7.4.7, 7.4.8 • **WS**: 7.3.4, 7.4.2	Emphasized are the following: • Reasoning • See things in the mind's eye • Integrity and honesty • Organize and maintain information	Emphasized are the following: • Provide for physical needs • Find and use community resources and services • Exercise human and legal rights and civic responsibilities • Help self and others	• **1**: 24.01 • **2**: 32.01 • **3**: 32.10 • **4**: 24.04, 27.02 • **5**: 23.01, 27.01 • **6**: 24.02 • **7**: 32.10, 32.13 • **WS**: 32.05, 32.08
• Recognize different types of housing in a community • Use classified ads as a source of community information	• Interpret bar graphs • Compare rent prices for apartments and houses • Interpret and pay bills	• **1**: 1.4.1 • **2**: 1.4.2 • **3**: 0.1.6, 3.4.2, 6.7.2 • **4**: 1.4.2 • **5**: 2.1.8, 2.2.1, 7.5.5 • **6**: 1.5.1, 1.5.3, 1.8.2, 2.4.1 • **7**: 0.1.2, 7.1.4, 7.4.7, 7.4.8 • **GS**: 0.2.1, 0.2.4	Emphasized are the following: • Decision making • See things in the mind's eye • Acquire and evaluate information	Emphasized are the following: • Find, interpret, and analyze diverse sources of information • Provide for physical needs • Find and use community resources and services	• **1**: 28.04 • **2**: 32.07 • **3**: 32.04 • **4**: 28.04 • **5**: 23.02 • **6**: 25.06, 28.05 • **7**: 32.13 • **GS**: 33.07
• Use help wanted ads as a source of community information • Recognize some dos and don'ts of interviewing	• Solve word problems • Understand hourly wages • Use addition and multiplication to calculate totals	• **1**: 4.1.6, 4.4.2, 6.6.5 • **2**: 4.4.4, 4.4.5, 4.4.6, 4.4.7 • **3**: 4.1.2, 4.1.5, 4.1.7 • **4**: 4.1.9 • **5**: 4.1.2, 4.1.7 • **6**: 4.1.2 • **7**: 0.1.2, 7.1.4, 7.4.7, 7.4.8 • **WS**: 7.5.2, 7.5.4	Emphasized are the following: • Problem solving • Self-esteem • Integrity and honesty • Acquire and evaluate information • Analyze and communicate information • Work within the system	Emphasized are the following: • Find and get a job • Plan and renew career goals • Find, interpret, and analyze diverse sources of information	• **1**: 32.01 • **2**: 18.02 • **3**: 20.02 • **4**: 32.02 • **5**: 18.02, 20.02 • **6**: 18.03 • **7**: 32.08, 32.13 • **WS**: 32.01, 32.10

CASAS and LCP standards: Numbers in bold indicate lesson numbers.   •   **GS**: Grammar Spotlight   •   **WS**: Writing Spotlight

All-Star is a four-level, standards-based series for English learners featuring a picture-dictionary approach to vocabulary building. "Big picture" scenes in each unit provide springboards to a wealth of activities developing all of the language skills.

An accessible and predictable sequence of lessons in each unit systematically builds language and math skills around life-skill topics. *All-Star* presents family, work, *and* community topics in each unit, and provides alternate application lessons in its Workbooks, giving teachers the flexibility to customize the series for a variety of student needs and curricular objectives. *All-Star* is tightly correlated to all of the major national and state standards for adult instruction.

Features

★ **Accessible "big picture" scenes** present life-skills vocabulary and provide engaging contexts for all-skills language development.

★ **Predictable sequence of eight, two-page lessons** in each unit reduces prep time for teachers and helps students get comfortable with the pattern of each lesson type.

★ **Flexible structure** allows teachers to customize each unit to meet a variety of student needs and curricular objectives, with application lessons addressing family, work, and community topics in both the Student Book and Workbook.

★ **Comprehensive coverage of key standards, such as CASAS, SCANS, EFF, and LCPs,** prepares students to master a broad range of critical competencies.

★ **Multiple assessment measures** like CASAS-style tests and performance-based assessment offer a broad range of options for monitoring and assessing learner progress.

★ **Dynamic, Interactive CD-ROM program** integrates language, literacy, and numeracy skill building with computer practice.

The Complete *All-Star* Program

★ The **Student Book** features ten, 16-page units, integrating listening, speaking, reading, writing, grammar, math, and pronunciation skills with life-skill topics, critical thinking activities, and civics concepts.

★ The **Student Book with Audio Highlights** provides students with audio recordings of all of the dialogs in the Student Book. This audio CD also includes recordings of all of the new vocabulary presented in the "big picture" scenes.

★ The **Teacher's Edition with Tests** provides:
  • Step-by-step procedural notes for each Student Book activity
  • 250 expansion activities for Student Book 1, many of which offer creative tasks tied to the "big picture" scenes in each unit
  • Culture, Grammar, and Pronunciation Notes
  • Two-page written test for each unit (*Note:* Listening passages for the tests are available on the Student Book Audiocassettes and Audio CDs.)
  • Audio scripts for all audio program materials
  • Answer keys for Student Book, Workbook, and Tests

★ The **Interactive CD-ROM** incorporates and extends the learning goals of the Student Book by integrating language, literacy, and numeracy skill building with multimedia practice on the computer. A flexible set of activities correlated to each unit builds vocabulary, listening, reading, writing, and test-taking skills.

★ The **Color Overhead Transparencies** encourage teachers to present new vocabulary and concepts in fun and meaningful ways. This component provides a full-color overhead transparency for each of the "big picture" scenes.

★ The **Workbook** includes supplementary practice activities correlated to the Student Book. As a bonus feature, the Workbook also includes alternate application lessons addressing the learner's role as worker, family member, and/or community member. These additional, optional lessons may be used in addition to, or as substitutes for, the application lessons found in Lesson 6 of each Student Book unit.

★ The **Audiocassettes** and **Audio CDs** contain recordings for all listening activities in the Student Book. Listening passages for each unit test are provided at the end of the audio section for that unit.

Overview of the *All-Star* Program

UNIT STRUCTURE

Consult the *Welcome to All-Star* guide on pages xiv–xix. This guide offers teachers and administrators a visual tour of one Student Book unit.

All-Star is designed to maximize accessibility and flexibility. Each unit contains the following sequence of eight, two-page lessons that develop vocabulary and build language, grammar, and math skills around life-skill topics:

★ Lesson 1: Vocabulary

★ Lesson 2: Vocabulary in Action

★ Lesson 3: Talk About It

★ Lesson 4: Reading and Writing

★ Lesson 5: Conversation

★ Lesson 6: Application

★ Lesson 7: Review and Assessment

★ Grammar or Writing Spotlight

Each lesson addresses a key adult standard, and these standards are indicated in the upper right-hand corner of each lesson in a yellow bar.

SPECIAL FEATURES OF EACH UNIT

★ *Window on Grammar.* Grammar is presented and practiced in each unit in blue boxes called *Windows on Grammar.* These short presentations offer students small, manageable chunks of grammar that correlate with a variety of national and state standards. *Window on Grammar* boxes provide for written and oral practice of new language structures and functions. Students and teachers will find additional, in-depth grammar practice in a series of two-page lessons called *Spotlight: Grammar* presented throughout the book. A comprehensive *Grammar Reference Guide* at the back of the book summarizes all of the structures and functions presented.

★ *Window on Math.* Learning basic math skills is critically important for success in school, on the job, and at home. As such, national and state standards for adult education mandate instruction in basic math skills. In each unit, a blue box called *Window on Math* is dedicated to helping students develop the functional numeracy skills they need for basic math work.

★ *Window on Pronunciation.* The culminating activity in Lesson 5 (*Conversation*) of each unit is featured in a blue box called *Window on Pronunciation*. This special feature has two major goals: (1) helping students hear and produce specific sounds, words, and minimal pairs of words so they become better listeners and speakers; and (2) addressing issues of stress, rhythm, and intonation so that the students' spoken English becomes more comprehensible.

★ *Spotlight: Grammar and Spotlight: Writing.* At the end of each unit, students and teachers will find either a *Grammar Spotlight* or a *Writing Spotlight*. These are optional, two-page lessons that offer a supplementary focus on grammar or writing skill development.

TWO-PAGE LESSON FORMAT

The lessons in *All-Star* are designed as two-page spreads. Lessons 5–7 and the Spotlights employ a standard textbook layout, but Lessons 1–4 follow an innovative format with a list of activities on the left-hand page of the spread and picture-dictionary visuals supporting these activities on the right-hand page. The list of activities, entitled *Things To Do*, allows students and teachers to take full advantage of the visuals in each lesson, inviting students to achieve a variety of learning goals with them.

"BIG PICTURE" SCENES

Each unit includes one "big picture" scene in either Lesson 2 or Lesson 3. This scene is the visual centerpiece of each unit, and serves as a springboard to a variety of activities provided in the Student Book, Teacher's Edition, Color Overhead Transparencies package, and Interactive CD-ROM program. In the Student Book, the "big picture" scene introduces key vocabulary and serves as a prompt for classroom discussion. The scenes feature characters with distinct personalities for students to enjoy, respond to, and talk about. There are also surprising elements for students to discover in each "big picture" scene.

The Teacher's Edition includes a variety of all-skills "Big Picture Expansion" activities that are tied to the Student Book scenes. For each unit, these expansion activities address listening, speaking, reading, writing, *and* grammar skill development, and allow teachers to customize their instruction to meet the language learning needs of each group of students.

In the Color Overhead Transparencies package, teachers will find transparencies of each "big picture" scene, which they can use to introduce the vocabulary and life-skill concepts in each unit. They can also use these transparencies to facilitate the "Big Picture Expansion" activities in the Teacher's Edition.

Finally, the Interactive CD-ROM program highlights an additional aspect of the "big picture" scenes in its listening activities. Students working with the CD-ROM program listen to a series of new conversations taking place between characters in the "big picture" scenes. They then work through a series of interactive activities based on these conversations and receive immediate feedback on their work.

CIVICS CONCEPTS

Many institutions focus direct attention on the importance of civics instruction for English language learners. Civics instruction encourages students to become active and informed community members. Throughout each *All-Star* unit, students and teachers will encounter *Try This* activities that introduce students to civics concepts and encourage community involvement. In addition, *Application* lessons provide activities that help students develop their roles as workers, parents, and citizens. Those lessons targeting the students' role as citizen encourage learners to become more active and informed members of their communities.

CASAS, SCANS, EFF, LCPs, AND OTHER STANDARDS

Teachers and administrators benchmark student progress against national and/or state standards for adult instruction. With this in mind, *All-Star* carefully integrates instructional elements from a wide range of standards including CASAS, SCANS, EFF, and the Literacy Completion Points (LCPs). Unit-by-unit correlations of these standards appear in the scope and sequence on pages iv–ix. Here is a brief overview of our approach to meeting the key national and state standards:

★ **CASAS.** Many U.S. states, including California, tie funding for adult education programs to student performance on the Comprehensive Adult Student Assessment System (CASAS). The CASAS (www.casas.org) competencies identify more than 300 essential skills that adults need in order to succeed in the classroom, workplace, and community. Examples of these skills include identifying or using appropriate non-verbal behavior in a variety of settings, responding appropriately to common personal information questions, and comparing price or quality to determine the best buys. *All-Star* comprehensively integrates all of the CASAS Life Skill Competencies throughout the four levels of the series. Level 1 addresses all of the CASAS Level A Life Skills test items on Test Forms 31, 32, 51, and 52.

★ **SCANS.** Developed by the United States Department of Labor, SCANS is an acronym for the Secretary's Commission on Achieving Necessary Skills (wdr.doleta.gov/SCANS/). SCANS competencies are workplace skills that help people compete more effectively in today's global economy. The following are examples of SCANS competencies: works well with others, acquires and evaluates information, and teaches others new skills. A variety of SCANS competencies is threaded throughout the activities in each unit of *All-Star*. The incorporation of these competencies recognizes both the intrinsic importance of teaching workplace skills and the fact that many adult students are already working members of their communities.

★ **EFF.** Equipped for the Future (EFF) is a set of standards for adult literacy and lifelong learning, developed by The National Institute for Literacy (www.nifl.gov). The organizing principle of EFF is that adults assume responsibilities in three major areas of life — as workers, as parents, and as citizens. These three areas of focus are called "role maps" in the EFF documentation. In the parent role map, for example, EFF highlights these and other responsibilities: participating in children's formal education and forming and maintaining supportive family relationships. Each *All-Star* unit addresses all three of the EFF role maps in its *Application* lessons. Lesson 6 in each Student Book unit includes one of the three application lessons for that unit. The remaining two application lessons are found in the corresponding Workbook unit.

★ **LCPs.** Florida and Texas document the advancement of learners in an adult program through their system of Literacy Completion Points (LCPs). *All-Star* Level 1 incorporates into its instruction the vast majority of standards at LCP Level B.

NUMBER OF HOURS OF INSTRUCTION

The *All-Star* program has been designed to accommodate the needs of adult classes with 70–180 hours of classroom instruction. Here are three recommended ways in which various components in the *All-Star* program can be combined to meet student and teacher needs.

★ **70–100 hours.** Teachers are encouraged to work through all of the Student Book materials, incorporating the *Grammar* and *Writing Spotlights* as time permits. The Color Overhead Transparencies can be used to introduce and/or review materials in each unit. Teachers should also look to the Teacher's Edition for teaching suggestions and testing materials as necessary.
Time per unit: 7–10 hours.

★ **100–140 hours.** In addition to working through all of the Student Book materials, teachers are encouraged to incorporate the Workbook and Interactive CD-ROM activities for supplementary practice.
Time per unit: 10–14 hours.

★ **140–180 hours.** Teachers and students working in an intensive instructional setting can take advantage of the wealth of expansion activities threaded through the Teacher's Edition to supplement the Student Book, Workbook, and Interactive CD-ROM materials.
Time per unit: 14–18 hours.

ASSESSMENT

The *All-Star* program offers teachers, students, and administrators the following wealth of resources for monitoring and assessing student progress and achievement:

★ **Standardized testing formats.** *All-Star* is correlated to the CASAS competencies and many other national and state standards for adult learning. Students have the opportunity to practice answering CASAS-style listening and reading questions in Lesson 7 of each unit (*What do you know?*), in Lesson 7 of the Workbook (*Practice Test*), and in the Interactive CD-ROM program. Students practice with the same item types and bubble-in answer sheets they encounter on CASAS and other standardized tests.

★ **Achievement tests.** The *All-Star* Teacher's Edition includes end-of-unit tests. These paper-and-pencil tests help students demonstrate how well they have learned the instructional content of the unit. Adult learners often show incremental increases in learning that are not always measured on the standardized tests. The achievement tests may demonstrate learning even in a short amount of instructional time. Twenty percent of each test includes questions that encourage students to apply more academic skills such as determining meaning from context, making inferences, and understanding main ideas. Practice with these question types will help prepare students who may want to enroll in academic classes.

★ **Performance-based assessment.** *All-Star* provides several ways to measure students' performance on productive tasks, including the *Writing Spotlights* and *Conversation Checks* that have corresponding rubrics in the Student Book to facilitate self-assessment. In addition, the Teacher's Edition suggests writing and speaking prompts that teachers can use for performance-based assessment. These prompts derive from the "big picture" scene in each unit and provide rich visual input as the basis for the speaking and writing tasks asked of the students.

★ **Portfolio assessment.** A portfolio is a collection of student work that can be used to show progress. Examples of work that the instructor or the student may submit in the portfolio include writing samples, speaking rubrics, audiotapes, videotapes, or projects. Every Student Book unit includes several *Try This* activities. These activities require critical thinking and small-group project work. As such, they can be included in a student's portfolio. The Teacher's Edition identifies activities that may be used as documentation for the secondary standards defined by the National Reporting System.

★ **Self-assessment.** Self-assessment is an important part of the overall assessment picture, as it promotes student involvement and commitment to the learning process. When encouraged to assess themselves, students take more control of their learning and are better able to connect the instructional content with their own goals. The Student Book includes *Learning Logs* at the end of each unit, which allow students to check off the vocabulary they have learned and skills they have acquired. The Workbook provides self-check boxes in each lesson, encouraging students to monitor their own progress on individual activities and across units.

★ **Other linguistic and non-linguistic outcomes.** Traditional testing often does not account for the progress made by adult learners with limited educational experience or low literacy levels. Such learners tend to take longer to make smaller language gains, so the gains they make in other areas are often more significant. These gains may be in areas such as self-esteem, goal clarification, learning skills, and access to employment, community involvement and further academic studies. The SCANS and EFF standards identify areas of student growth that are not necessarily language based. *All-Star* is correlated with both SCANS and EFF standards. Every unit in the student book contains a lesson that focuses on one of the EFF role maps (worker, family member, community member), and the Workbook provides alternate lessons that address the other two role maps. Like the Student Book, the Workbook includes activities that may provide documentation that can be added to a student portfolio.

About the author and series consultants

Linda Lee is lead author on the *All-Star* series. Linda has taught ESL/ELT in the United States, Iran, and China, and has authored or co-authored a variety of successful textbook series for English learners. As a classroom instructor, Linda's most satisfying teaching experiences have been with adult ESL students at Roxbury Community College in Boston, Massachusetts.

Stephen Sloan is Title One Coordinator at James Monroe High School in the Los Angeles Unified School District. Steve has more than 25 years of teaching and administrative experience with both high school and adult ESL learners. Steve is also the author of McGraw-Hill's *Rights and Responsibilities: Reading and Communication for Civics*.

Grace Tanaka is professor and coordinator of ESL at the Santa Ana College School of Continuing Education, in Santa Ana, California, which serves more than 20,000 students per year. She is also a textbook co-author and series consultant. Grace has 23 years of teaching experience in both credit and non-credit ESL programs.

Shirley Velasco is assistant principal at Palmetto Adult Education Center in Miami, Florida. She has been a classroom instructor and administrator for the past 24 years. At Palmetto, Shirley has created a large adult ESOL program based on a curriculum she developed to help teachers implement the Florida LCPs (Literacy Completion Points).

Welcome to All-Star

All-Star is a four-level series featuring a "big picture" approach to meeting adult standards that systematically builds language and math skills around life-skill topics.

Predictable unit structure includes the same logical sequence of eight two-page lessons in each unit.

Accessible, two-page lesson format follows an innovative layout with a list of activities labeled "Things To Do" on the left and picture-dictionary visuals on the right.

Comprehensive coverage of key standards such as CASAS, SCANS, EFF, and LCPs prepares students to master critical competencies.

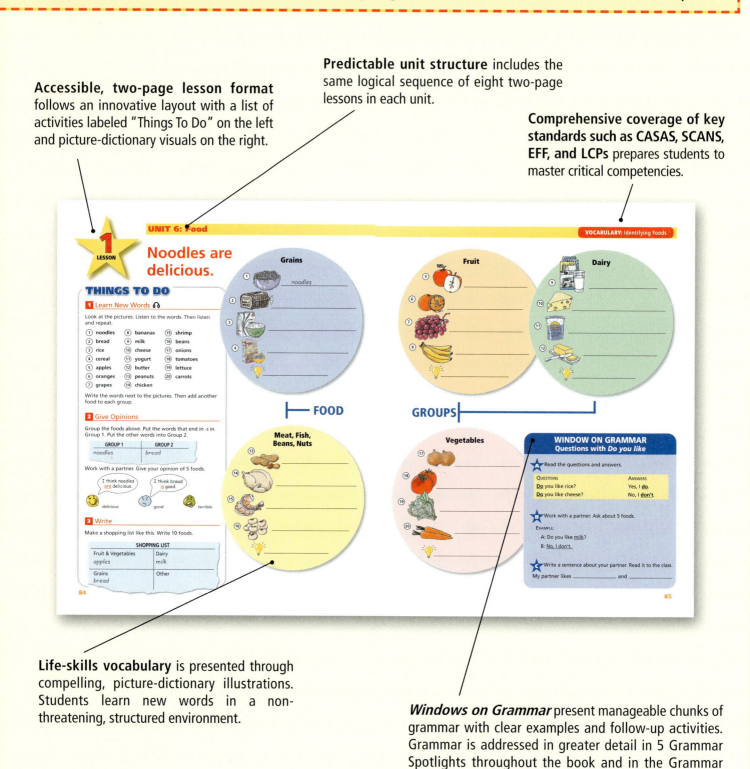

Life-skills vocabulary is presented through compelling, picture-dictionary illustrations. Students learn new words in a non-threatening, structured environment.

Windows on Grammar present manageable chunks of grammar with clear examples and follow-up activities. Grammar is addressed in greater detail in 5 Grammar Spotlights throughout the book and in the Grammar Reference Guide at the back of the book.

"Big picture" scenes are springboards to a wealth of all-skills expansion activities in the Teacher's Edition and Interactive CD-ROM.

Color overhead transparencies for the "big picture" scenes provide fun and meaningful ways to present new vocabulary and concepts.

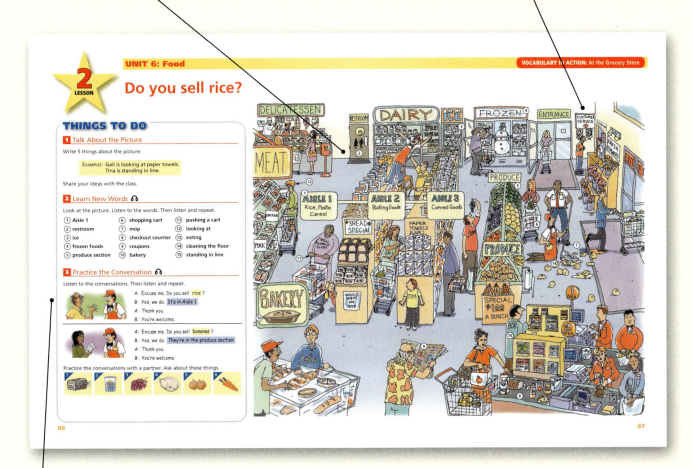

Structured speaking activities invite students to discuss the picture dictionary scene, simulate real-life conversations, and express their thoughts and opinions.

Reading activities develop critical thinking skills by asking students to find important information and make inferences.

Realia-based readings and narrative selections like maps, advertisements, descriptive paragraphs, and short stories provide the basis for developing reading skills.

Abundant opportunities for writing prepare students for a variety of academic and real-world writing challenges, such as completing standard forms and writing complete sentences.

Try This activities promote civics concepts by connecting classroom learning to community experiences.

Windows on Math help students build numeracy skills for basic math work.

Practice the Conversation activities invite students to engage in everyday conversations with their classmates, using the vocabulary and grammar they have learned.

Windows on Pronunciation help students produce difficult sounds in English and address issues of stress, rhythm, and intonation.

Interactive CD-ROM program incorporates and extends the learning goals of each Student Book unit by integrating language, literacy, and numeracy skill building with computer practice.

Application lessons focus on developing the students' roles in life as workers, parents, and citizens.

Real-world documents and situations are highlighted in the *Application* lessons, exposing students to critical concepts they encounter at work, at home, and in the community.

Alternate application lessons in the Workbook provide a flexible approach to addressing family, work, *and* community topics in each unit.

Listening Reviews help teachers assess listening comprehension, while giving students practice with the item types and answer sheets they encounter on standardized tests.

Conversation Checks are communicative information gap activities that also provide informal listening and speaking self-assessment tools.

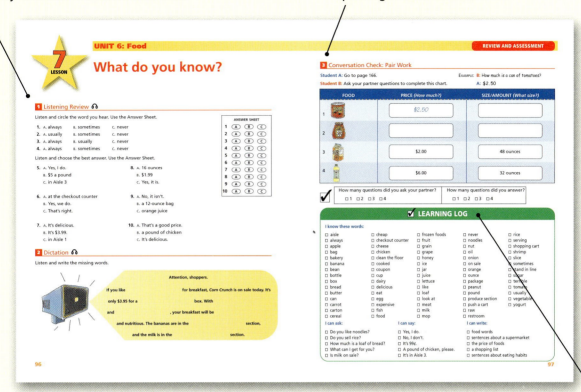

A Grammar or **Writing Spotlight** appears at the end of each unit, offering supplementary grammar or writing skill development.

Learning Logs ask students to catalog the vocabulary, grammar, and life skills they have learned, and determine which areas they need to review.

INTRODUCTION

What's your name?

1 Practice the Conversation 🎧

Listen to the conversation. Then listen and repeat.

A: Hello. My name is Anna .

B: Hi. I'm Tom .

A: Nice to meet you, Tom .

B: Nice to meet you, too.

Practice the conversation with 3 classmates.

2 Say the Alphabet 🎧

Listen to the letters. Then listen and repeat.

A a	B b	C c	D d
E e	F f	G g	H h
I i	J j	K k	L l
M m	N n	O o	P p
Q q	R r	S s	T t
U u	V v	W w	X x
Y y	Z z		

3 Practice the Conversation 🎧

Listen to the conversation. Then listen and repeat.

A: What's your first name?
B: Sue .
A: What's your last name?
B: Chan .
A: How do you spell that?
B: C-h-a-n .

Ask 6 classmates. Write their answers below.

FIRST NAME (GIVEN NAME)	LAST NAME (FAMILY NAME)
Sue	Chan

4 Write

Read Sue's name tag. Make a name tag for yourself.

Hi. My name is

Sue Chan

Hi. My name is

3

Where are you from?

LESSON 1

THINGS TO DO

1 Find the Countries 🎧

Look at the map. Listen to the words. Then listen and repeat.

① Canada
② the United States
③ Mexico
④ Haiti
⑤ Colombia
⑥ Brazil
⑦ France
⑧ Morocco
⑨ Somalia
⑩ China
⑪ Vietnam
⑫ _____

Write the name of one more country. Find it on the map.

2 Ask Questions 🎧

Listen to the conversation. Then listen and repeat.

A: What's your name?

B: My name is Victor .

A: Where are you from?

B: I am from Mexico .

A: Mexico ! That's interesting.

Ask 4 classmates: What's your name? Where are you from? Write their answers below.

WHAT'S YOUR NAME?	WHERE ARE YOU FROM?
Victor	Mexico

3 Write

Write about 4 classmates.

EXAMPLE: _Victor_ is from _Mexico_ .

★ ★

TRY THIS Name a country that begins with each letter of the alphabet.

EXAMPLE: A: Australia
B: Brazil
C: _____

★ ★

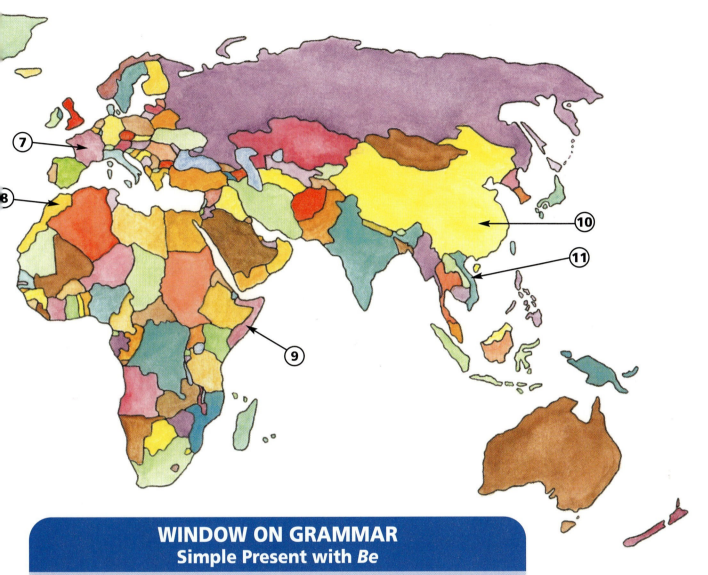

WINDOW ON GRAMMAR
Simple Present with *Be*

A Read the sentences.

I **am** from China.	You **are** from Japan.	He **is** from Brazil.
	We **are** from Haiti.	She **is** from France.
	They **are** from Mexico.	It **is** from Canada.

B Complete the sentences with *am, is,* or *are*.

1. Victor _____ from Mexico.
2. Victor and I _____ from Mexico.
3. Sandra _____ from Colombia.
4. I _____ from Vietnam.
5. You _____ from Somalia.
6. New York _____ in the United States.

5

LESSON 2

Where's your notebook?

THINGS TO DO

1 Learn New Words 🎧

Look at the picture. Listen to the words. Then listen and repeat.

① teacher	⑥ table	⑪ pencil	⑮ chair
② wall	⑦ calendar	⑫ piece of paper	⑯ computer
③ clock	⑧ map		⑰ desk
④ door	⑨ notebook	⑬ book	⑱ student
⑤ board	⑩ pen	⑭ floor	⑲ window

2 Write

What's in your classroom? Write 5 things. Then share your ideas with the class.

clock _____   _____

_____   _____

_____   _____

3 Ask Questions

Work with a partner. Ask and answer questions about the picture.

A: Where's

the map?	the computer?
the book?	the _____?

B: It's

on the wall.	on the table.
on the desk.	_____.

★★★★★★★★★★★★★★★★★★★★★★★★★★

 TRY THIS Make vocabulary flash cards like this.

(Front) (Back) chair

Use your flash cards to learn new words.

★★★★★★★★★★★★★★★★★★★★★★★★★★

Ali

Jane

3 LESSON

Read page 6.

THINGS TO DO

1 Learn New Words 🎧

Look at the pictures. Listen to the classroom instructions. Then listen and repeat.

2 Follow Instructions

Work with a partner. Take turns giving 5 instructions.

A: Raise your hand.

3 Write

Write your own instructions. Then give an instruction to the class.

1. Say hello.
2. Write _____
3. Open _____
4. Close _____
5. Go to _____

★★★★★★★★★★★★★★★★★★★★★★★★★★★★★

TRY THIS Make a diagram like this. Add words to it.

Things that open and close

door

★★★★★★★★★★★★★★★★★★★★★★★★★★★★★

① Read page 10.

② Listen to the words.

⑦ Write your name.

⑧ Practice the conversation with a partner.

⑬ Stand up.

⑭ Sit down.

③ Repeat the words.

④ Say *computer*.

⑤ Ask a partner.

⑥ Circle your name.

⑨ Take out a piece of paper.

⑩ Open your book.

⑪ Close the window.

⑫ Raise your hand.

⑮ Go to the board.

WINDOW ON MATH 🎧
Numbers 0 to 11

⭐ A Listen to the numbers. Then listen and repeat.

0	1	2	3
zero	one	two	three
4	5	6	7
four	five	six	seven
8	9	10	11
eight	nine	ten	eleven

⭐ B Listen to the conversation. Then listen and repeat.

A: Open your book to page 5.
B: Which page?
A: Page 5.

Practice the conversation with a partner.
Use different numbers.

9

Application Forms

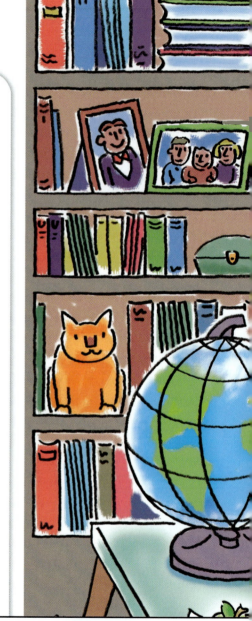

THINGS TO DO

1 Learn New Words 🎧

Look at the picture. Listen to the information. Then listen and repeat.

1. middle name
2. address
3. street
4. city
5. state
6. zip code
7. telephone number
8. area code
9. birthplace
10. gender
11. male
12. female
13. marital status
14. single
15. married
16. divorced
17. occupation

2 Read

Read the application form. Complete the sentences below.

Paul's _____*last*_____ _____*name*_____ is Bridges. His

_____ _____ is Richard. His _____ is

8517 Alvarado Street in Los Angeles, California. The _____

_____ is 91012. Paul's _____ _____

is (310) 555-5678. His _____ is the U.S.

3 Write

Work with a partner.

Ask questions.

Write your partner's answers on the form.

EXAMPLE: What's your <u>first name</u>?

Application Form

Name _____
       First   Middle   Last

Address _____
         Street   City   State   Zip Code

Telephone Number _____
                   Area Code

Birthplace _____

Gender: ☐ Male ☐ Female Marital Status: ☐ Single ☐ Married ☐ Divorced

Occupation _____

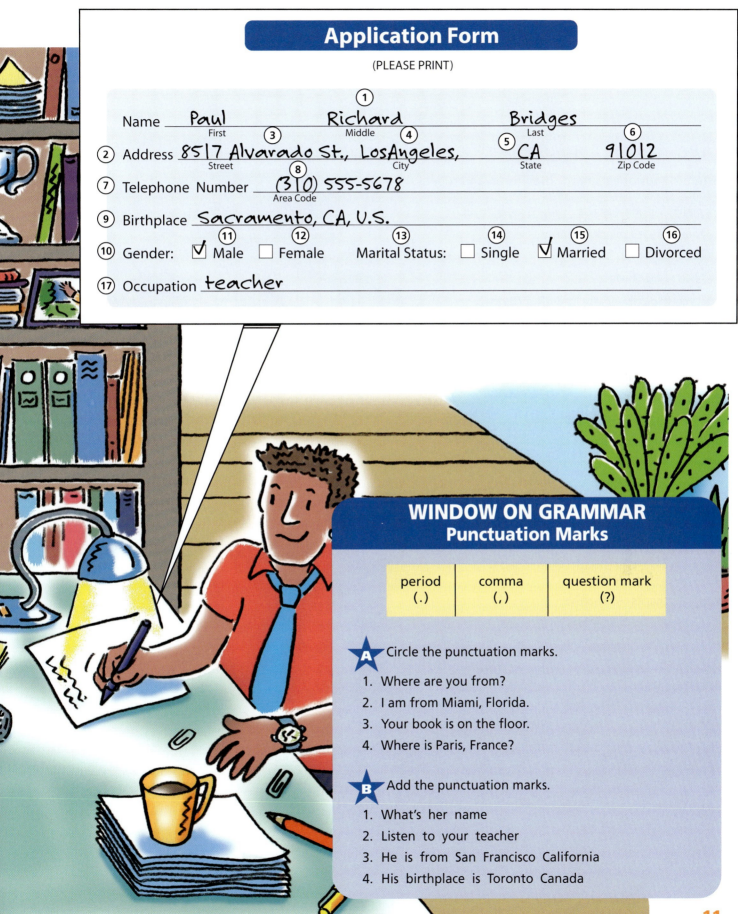

Application Form

(PLEASE PRINT)

Name ① Paul *First*   Richard *Middle*   Bridges *Last*

② Address 8517 Alvarado St., ③ *Street* LosAngeles, ④ *City* ⑤ CA *State* ⑥ 91012 *Zip Code*

⑦ Telephone Number ⑧ (310) *Area Code* 555-5678

⑨ Birthplace Sacramento, CA, U.S.

⑩ Gender: ⑪ ☑ Male   ⑫ ☐ Female   Marital Status: ⑬ ☐ Single   ⑮ ☑ Married   ⑯ ☐ Divorced

⑭

⑰ Occupation teacher

WINDOW ON GRAMMAR
Punctuation Marks

period (.)	comma (,)	question mark (?)

A Circle the punctuation marks.

1. Where are you from?
2. I am from Miami, Florida.
3. Your book is on the floor.
4. Where is Paris, France?

B Add the punctuation marks.

1. What's her name
2. Listen to your teacher
3. He is from San Francisco California
4. His birthplace is Toronto Canada

11

5 LESSON

Nice to meet you.

1 Practice the Conversation: Greeting Someone 🎧

Listen to the conversation. Then listen and repeat.

A: Hello . I'm Mr. Campos.

B: Nice to meet you, Mr. Campos.
I'm Ms. Jones .

A: Nice to meet you.

Practice the conversation with a partner.
Use these items.

1	Hi.	2	How do you do?
	Mrs. Lee		Mrs. Bridges

3	Hello.	4	How do you do?
	Ms. Kim		Mr. Thomas

> Mr. = a single or married male
> Ms. = a single or married female
> Mrs. = a married female

2 Practice the Conversation: Introducing Someone 🎧

Listen to the conversation. Then listen and repeat.

A: Hi, Jon. How are you?

B: Fine , thanks. And you?

A: I'm fine. Jon, this is my friend Gina.

B: Hi, Gina. Nice to meet you.

Practice the conversation with a partner.
Use these items.

1 Good	2 Not bad	3 OK	4 Great
I want to introduce you to	I want you to meet	this is	I want you to meet

3 Practice the Conversation: Saying Good-bye

Listen to the conversation. Then listen and repeat.

A: Good-bye, Jon.

B: Bye, David. Have a nice day.

A: You too.

Practice the conversation with a partner.
Use these items.

1 See you later.	**2** Nice to see you.	**3** Have a great day.	**4** Have a good day.
Have a nice day.	Nice to see you, too.	OK, you too.	Thanks, you too.

WINDOW ON PRONUNCIATION
Long Vowel Sounds: *I* and *E*

A Listen to the words. Then listen and repeat.

1. I	4. me	7. my	10. he	13. we	16. read
2. fine	5. meet	8. try	11. street	14. write	17. bye
3. see	6. hi	9. three	12. China	15. nice	18. country

B Write the words in the correct place.

Sounds like *I*		Sounds like *E*	
I	_____	see	_____
fine	_____	me	_____
_____	_____	_____	_____
_____	_____	_____	_____
_____	_____	_____	_____

C Listen and circle the word you hear.

1. (my)	me	3. I	E	5. bye	B
2. hi	he	4. write	read	6. Y	we

Occupations

1 Learn New Words 🎧

Look at the pictures below. Listen to the words. Then listen and repeat.

① Joan Baxter is a **dentist**.

② Larry Fisher is a **bus driver**.

③ Ken Park is a **pharmacist**.

④ Emma Lambert is a **doctor**.

⑤ Paul Ming is a **salesclerk**.

⑥ David Campos is a **machinist**.

⑦ Gina Mata is a **police officer**.

⑧ Leo Brunov is a **nurse**.

⑨ Amy Craft is a **cashier**.

2 Ask Questions

Work with a partner. Ask about the people above.

A: What's Joan's occupation?

B: She's a dentist.

Possessives
Add 's to a
person's name.

3 Read

Read the ads and circle the occupations.

JOB ADS

1 *4 Day Work Week* **BUS DRIVER** Earn $14/hr Please call 916–555–0819 for an interview.	**2** Immediate Openings for 3 Machinists Apply at: J&D Machine Co. 433 Ray Avenue Auburn, California 916–202–1234	**3** SALESCLERK Experienced. Must Work Weekends. Food for Pets. 11 Alvarado Street 555–7400
4 CASHIER WANTED Work 3 days a week. Apply in person: Shop and Go 873 Mission Street 916–682–1414	**5** Smith Drugstore needs a Pharmacist for their Sacramento store. Call for an interview: 916–555–8700	**6** DRIVER, Tow Truck full time. Must live in Davis, experience necessary. 10 Johnson Road 916–555–0612

4 Write

Write the occupations. Then write the street address or telephone number from each job ad.

	OCCUPATION	STREET ADDRESS	TELEPHONE NUMBER
1.	Bus driver	XXX	(916) 555-0819
2.			
3.			
4.			
5.			
6.			

UNIT 1: Getting Started

What do you know?

1 Listening Review 🎧

Listen and choose the correct answer. Use the Answer Sheet below.

1.

A   B   C

2.

A   B   C

3.

A   B   C

4.

A   B   C

5. A. 22 Long Street
   B. 555-5498
   C. 03550

6. A. 212
   B. 54356
   C. 555-5683

7. A. She's from Haiti.
   B. female
   C. She's a police officer.

8. A. Los Angeles
   B. California
   C. Mexico

9. A. 22
   B. 508
   C. 555-2494

10. A. 10 Main Street
    B. 423
    C. 555-5428

ANSWER SHEET		
1 (A)	(B)	(C)
2 (A)	(B)	(C)
3 (A)	(B)	(C)
4 (A)	(B)	(C)
5 (A)	(B)	(C)
6 (A)	(B)	(C)
7 (A)	(B)	(C)
8 (A)	(B)	(C)
9 (A)	(B)	(C)
10 (A)	(B)	(C)

2 Conversation Check: Pair Work

Student A: Go to page 164.

Student B: Ask your partner questions to complete this chart. Write the answers.

EXAMPLE: **B:** What is Don's last name?
A: Garcia.

	First Name	Last Name	Gender	Occupation	Telephone Number
1.	Don	*Garcia*	M	Police Officer	(545) 555-5943
2.	Gloria	Ramos	F	Nurse	
3.	Van	Pham	F		(943) 555-5873
4.		Smith	M	Cashier	(543) 555-9004
5.	Victor	Abarca	M		(359) 555-4833

✔

How many questions did you ask your partner?	How many questions did you answer?
□ 1　□ 2　□ 3　□ 4　□ 5	□ 1　□ 2　□ 3　□ 4　□ 5

✔ LEARNING LOG

I know these words:

□ address	□ country	□ male	□ period	□ student
□ am	□ dentist	□ map	□ pharmacist	□ table
□ are	□ desk	□ marital status	□ piece of paper	□ take out
□ area code	□ divorced	□ married	□ police officer	□ teacher
□ ask	□ doctor	□ middle name	□ practice	□ telephone
□ birthplace	□ door	□ Mr.	□ question mark	number
□ board	□ eight	□ Mrs.	□ raise	□ ten
□ book	□ eleven	□ Ms.	□ read	□ three
□ bus driver	□ female	□ nine	□ repeat	□ two
□ calendar	□ fine	□ notebook	□ salesclerk	□ wall
□ cashier	□ five	□ nurse	□ say	□ window
□ chair	□ floor	□ occupation	□ seven	□ write
□ circle	□ four	□ one	□ single	□ zero
□ city	□ gender	□ open	□ sit down	□ zip code
□ clock	□ go to	□ partner	□ six	
□ close	□ is	□ pen	□ stand up	
□ comma	□ listen	□ pencil	□ state	
□ computer	□ machinist	□ people	□ street	

I can ask:

□ What's your name?
□ Where are you from?
□ Where's your book?
□ How do you do?

I can say:

□ I am from Mexico.
□ That's interesting!
□ It's on the table.
□ Open your book.
□ This is my friend, Gina.
□ Have a nice day.

I can write:

□ personal information
□ telephone numbers
□ zip codes
□ street addresses
□ numbers 0 to 11

Spotlight: Grammar

SIMPLE PRESENT OF *BE*		
Affirmative	Negative	Contractions Affirmative Negative
I **am** from China.	I **am not** from China.	I'm I'm not
You **are** from China. We **are** from China. They **are** from China.	You **are not** from China. We **are not** from China. They **are not** from China.	You're You aren't We're We aren't They're They aren't
He **is** from China. She **is** from China. It **is** from China.	He **is not** from China. She **is not** from China. It **is not** from China.	He's He isn't She's She isn't It's It isn't

1   Read the story. Circle 16 examples of the simple present of *be*.

There are twenty (20) students in my class. Ten students are from Mexico. Four students are from Russia. Three students are from China. Two students are from Haiti, and one student is from Egypt. Eleven students in my class are married. Nine students are single. I am the student from Egypt. My name is Fatima, and I am married. My teacher is Mr. White. His first name is David, and he is from Canada. Mr. White is not married. He is single.

2   Read the story again. Complete the sentences with *are, is, are not,* and *is not*.

1. Fatima _____*is not*_____ from Russia. She _____*is*_____ from Egypt.

2. Fatima _____ married. She _____ single.

3. Eleven students in Fatima's class _____ married.

4. Mr. White _____ a bus driver. He _____ a teacher.

5. Mr. White and Fatima _____ from the United States.

6. Mr. White _____ from Egypt. He _____ from Canada.

7. Two students in Fatima's class _____ from Haiti.

3   Rewrite each sentence above. Use contractions.

EXAMPLE: *Fatima isn't from Russia. She's from Egypt.*

POSSESSIVE ADJECTIVES: *my, your, our, their, her, his*

my book	your book	our book	their book	her book	his book

POSSESSIVES WITH NAMES

John's book is here.

Tina's book is on the table.

Mr. White's book is on the desk.

John and Tina's teacher is Mr. White.

Andy's address is on the application form.

Ms. Jones's zip code is 94704.

4 Complete the sentences. Write *my, your, our, their, his,* or *her.*

1. Ling and Bob live in Pasadena. _____*Their*_____ address is 5434 N. Wilson Avenue.

2. Tina and I are students. _____ school is on Altadena Drive.

3. My teacher's first name is John. _____ middle name is Frank.

4. I live in New York. _____ telephone number is (212) 555-5439.

5. Anna is not married. _____ marital status is single.

6. Mr. Santos and Ms. Jones are teachers. _____ students are in _____ classrooms.

5 Write a sentence about each person.

1. Bob/telephone number/555-9584

   Bob's telephone number is 555-9584.

2. David/zip code/91012

   _____

3. Rose/marital status/married

   _____

4. Anna/area code/212

   _____

5. Mr. White/first name/David

   _____

Where's the post office?

Public Services

THINGS TO DO

1 Learn New Words 🎧

Look at the pictures. Listen to the words. Then listen and repeat.

1. fire station
2. police station
3. post office
4. community center
5. library
6. bookmobile
7. school
8. park
9. bank
10. drugstore
11. gas station
12. supermarket
13. hospital
14. laundromat
15. movie theater
16. restaurant

2 Practice the Conversation 🎧

Look at the Westville telephone book.
Listen to the conversation. Then listen and repeat.

A: Where's the community center ?

B: It's on Daniel Street .

A: What's the phone number?

B: It's area code 643-555-1547 .

A: Thanks.

B: You're welcome.

WESTVILLE

WESTVILLE, CITY OF —
Community Center
  1135 Daniel Street.....................643-555-1547
Fire Station
  1170 High Street.......................643-555-1639
Library
  118 Low Street..........................643-555-4887
School, Adams
  154 State Street........................643-555-4600

UNITED STATES GOVERNMENT
Post Office
  Westville Downtown office —
  80 Main Street...........................643-555-1300

Practice the conversation with a partner. Ask about the fire station, library, school, and post office.

★★★★★★★★★★★★★★★★★★★★★★★★★★★★★★★

 TRY THIS List 5 places in your area. Write the address and telephone number for each place.

★★★★★★★★★★★★★★★★★★★★★★★★★★★★★★★

20

Businesses

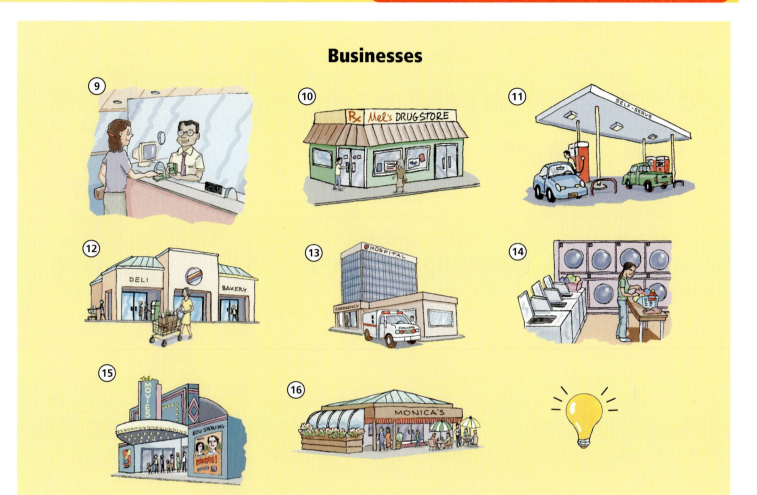

WINDOW ON GRAMMAR
There is/There are

A Read the sentences.

> **There is** a fire station on High Street.
> **There is** a post office on Main Street.
> **There are** two supermarket**s** on Low Street.
> **There are** three gas station**s** in town.

B Complete the sentences with *is* or *are*.

1. There _____ six movie theaters in town.
2. There _____ a supermarket on Daniel Street.
3. There _____ two schools on State Street.
4. There _____ a community center in town.

C Write 3 sentences about your street or town. Use *There is* or *There are*.

LESSON 2

It's next to the drugstore.

THINGS TO DO

1 Learn New Words 🎧

Look at the pictures. Listen to the words. Then listen and repeat.

1. next to
2. between
3. across from
4. in front of
5. near
6. in back of
7. on the corner of

Write the words on the pictures.

2 Practice the Conversation 🎧

Listen to the conversation. Then listen and repeat.

A: Excuse me. Where's the post office ?

B: It's next to the drugstore .

A: Next to the drugstore ?

B: That's right.

Practice the conversation with a partner. Ask about each picture.

3 Write

Work with a partner. Find the places in pictures 1 to 7 on the map.

EXAMPLE: The post office is here.

★★★★★★★★★★★★★★★★★★★★★★★★★★★★★★★★★

TRY THIS — Make a map of the area around your school. For example, draw the street and identify 5 buildings.

★★★★★★★★★★★★★★★★★★★ Places ★★★★★★★★★

The post office is ___next___ ___to___ the drugstore.

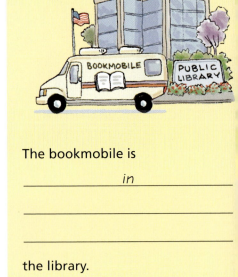

The bookmobile is _____ ___in___ _____ _____ the library.

There's a park _____ ___in___ _____ _____ the library.

The laundromat is _____

the drugstore and the supermarket.

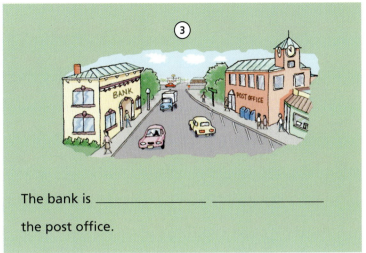

The bank is _____ _____

the post office.

The school is _____

the park.

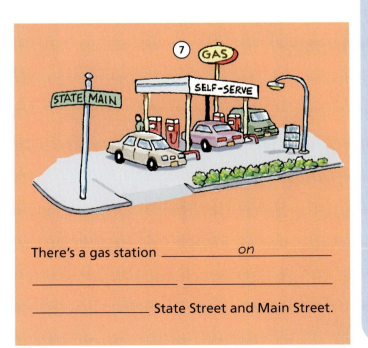

There's a gas station _____ *on*

_____ _____

_____ State Street and Main Street.

WINDOW ON GRAMMAR
Is there/Are there

A Read the sentences.

QUESTIONS	ANSWERS
Is there a bank on Third Street?	Yes, there is.
Is there a school on Third Street?	No, there isn't.
Are there parks in town?	Yes, there are.
Are there movie theaters in town?	No, there aren't.

B Complete the sentences with *Is there* or *Are there*. Then ask a partner.

1. _____ a supermarket near your home?

2. _____ a community center near your home?

3. _____ gas stations in your town?

4. _____ a bank across from your home?

5. _____ good restaurants near your home?

6. _____ two movie theaters on your street?

3 LESSON

Is there an ATM around here?

THINGS TO DO

1 Talk About the Picture

Write 5 things about the picture. Share your ideas with the class.

EXAMPLES: There's a post office on Pine Street.
There's a restaurant next to the drugstore.

2 Learn New Words 🎧

Look at the picture. Listen to the words. Then listen and repeat.

① bus stop   ⑧ stoplight   ⑮ no parking
② parking lot   ⑨ truck   ⑯ do not enter
③ bus   ⑩ taxi   ⑰ no right turn
④ ambulance   ⑪ car   ⑱ no left turn
⑤ crosswalk   ⑫ pay phone   ⑲ one way
⑥ sidewalk   ⑬ ATM
⑦ mailbox   ⑭ stop

3 Practice the Conversation 🎧

Listen to the conversation. Then listen and repeat.

A: Excuse me. Is there a mailbox around here?

B: Yes, there is. There's one on Pine Street. It's in front of the post office.

A: Thanks a lot.

Practice the conversation with a partner. Ask about these things.

in front of / ?

in front of / ?

next to / ?

near / ?

between / ?

across from / ?

25

Maps

4 LESSON

Washington

Oregon

Idaho

Nevada

① Sacramento

Utah

California

Arizona

Hawaii

Alaska

THINGS TO DO

1 Talk About the Picture

Answer the questions.

QUESTIONS	ANSWERS
a. What states are next to Florida?	*Alabama and Georgia*
b. What states are next to California?	
c. What state is between Texas and Arizona?	
d. Where is the city of Atlanta?	

Write 3 questions about places in the U.S. Ask a partner your questions.

2 Learn New Words 🎧

Look at the map. Listen to the words. Then listen and repeat.

① capital   ③ south of   ⑤ west of

② north of   ④ east of

Write the words on the lines below.

1. The _____*capital*_____ of Florida is Tallahassee.
2. New York is _____ Pennsylvania.
3. Texas is _____ Oklahoma.
4. Texas is _____ New Mexico.
5. Arizona is _____ New Mexico.

3 Read

Read and answer the questions.

1.	2.
This state is north of Alabama and south of Kentucky. The capital of this state is Nashville. What state is it?	This state is east of Utah and west of Kansas. The capital of this state is Denver. What state is it?
_____	_____

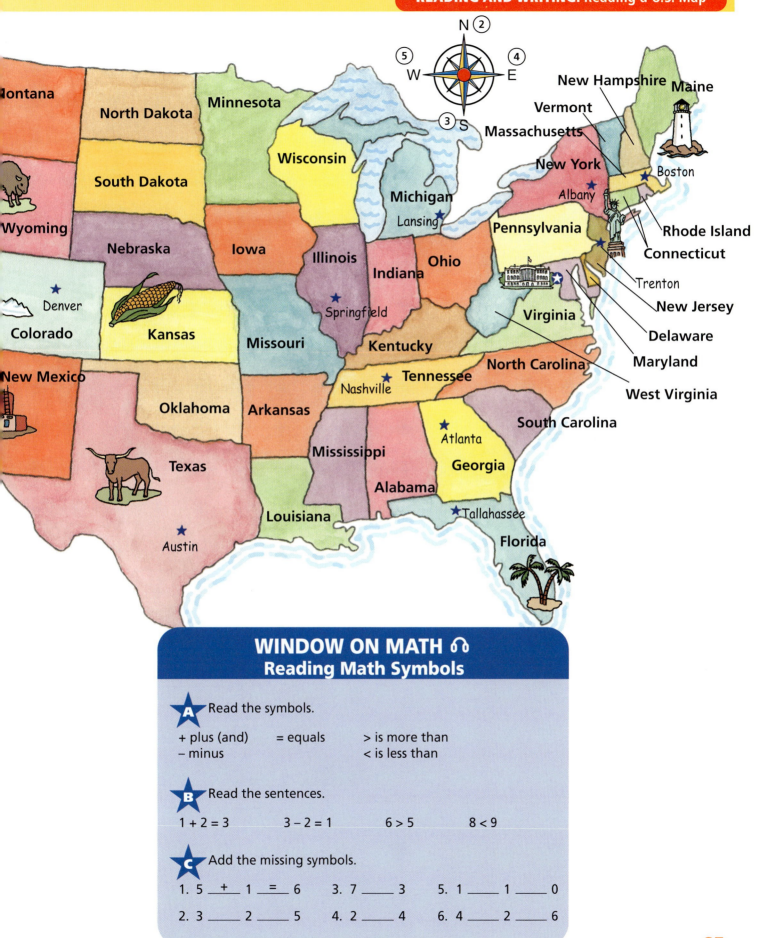

WINDOW ON MATH 🎧
Reading Math Symbols

A Read the symbols.

+ plus (and)   = equals   > is more than
– minus   < is less than

B Read the sentences.

1 + 2 = 3   3 – 2 = 1   6 > 5   8 < 9

C Add the missing symbols.

1. 5 __+__ 1 __=__ 6   3. 7 _____ 3   5. 1 _____ 1 _____ 0

2. 3 _____ 2 _____ 5   4. 2 _____ 4   6. 4 _____ 2 _____ 6

5 LESSON

Is there a restaurant near here?

1 Practice the Conversation: Asking for Repetition 🎧

Listen to the conversation. Then listen and repeat.

A: Is there a restaurant near here?
B: Excuse me?
A: Is there a restaurant near here?
B: Yes, there is. There's one on Pine.
A: Thanks.

Practice the conversation with a partner. Use these items.

1 a supermarket	2 an ATM	3 a bank	4
I'm sorry, what was that?	Please say that again.	What was that?	

2 Practice the Conversation: Saying You Don't Know 🎧

Listen to the conversation. Then listen and repeat.

A: Excuse me. Is there a drugstore near here?
B: I'm not sure.
A: Okay. Thanks anyway.

Practice the conversation with a partner. Use these items.

1 a gas station	2 a parking lot	3 a laundromat	4
Sorry, I don't know.	Sorry, I'm new in town.	Sorry, I'm not sure.	

3 Practice the Conversation: Asking a Follow-Up Question 🎧

Listen to the conversation. Then listen and repeat.

A: Where's Sacramento ?

B: It's in California .

A: In the north or south of the state?

B: In the north .

Practice the conversation with a partner. Use these items.

1 Atlanta

Georgia/north

2 Tallahassee

Florida/north

3 Lansing

Michigan/?

4 💡

WINDOW ON PRONUNCIATION 🎧
Voiced and Voiceless *Th* Sounds

 A Listen to the words. Then listen and repeat.

1. thanks	3. there	5. theater	7. three	9. the	11. they
2. then	4. third	6. that	8. this	10. north	12. south

Write the words in the correct place.

Th sounds like *thanks*		*Th* sounds like *the*	
thanks		the	

 B Work with a partner. Ask and answer the questions.

1. What is 1 plus 2?

2. Is there a bank near the school?

3. Is the United States north or south of Mexico?

4. Is the United States north or south of Canada?

5. Where is the theater?

The Public Library

1 Learn New Words 🎧

Look at the pictures. Listen to the words. Then listen and repeat.

1. **librarian**
2. **checkout desk**
3. **library card**
4. **magazines**
5. **audiobooks**
6. **videos**
7. **children's books**

Write the words on the lines.

1 *librarian* _____

2 _____

3 _____

No. _____ Name _____

Edwards Public Library
42 Linsdale Ave.
Springfield, Illinois

Present this card each time you borrow a book.
You are responsible for books borrowed on this card.

How do I get a library card?
Go to the checkout desk and complete
an application. Your card is free.

4 _____

5 _____

6 _____

What can I take out from the library?
You can take out books, magazines,
audiobooks, and videos.

What's in the library for children?
There are lots of books for children. There is also a story-telling program.

⑦ _____

Are there any computers in the library?
Yes, there are. You can use the computers in the library.

2 Write

Complete this library card application form.

🏛 Edwards Public Library

Application for an Adult Library Card

Part 1   Please print clearly. Enter only one letter or number per box.

Last Name

First Name   Middle Name or Initial

Street Address   Apt.#

City   State   Zip Code

Area Code   Phone Number   Email address

Part 2   Please choose an easy-to-remember four-digit Personal Identification Number (PIN).

Numbers only, no letters.

Part 3   Please read the statement and then sign your name.

I agree to be responsible for all materials borrowed against my Edwards Public Library card. I will notify the library immediately if my address changes or if my card is lost.

_____
Signature

★★★★★★★★★★★★★★★★★★★★★★★★★★★★★★★★

TRY THIS

Go to your public library. Write 5 things you see.

★★★★★★★★★★★★★★★★★★★★★★★★★★★★★★★★

⭐ 7 LESSON

What do you know?

1 Listening Review 🎧

Listen and choose the correct place. Use the Answer Sheet.

1. A. the police station
   B. the drugstore
   C. the fire station

2. A. the bank
   B. the fire station
   C. the supermarket

3. A. the drugstore
   B. the fire station
   C. the library

4. A. the police station
   B. the bank
   C. the supermarket

5. A. the hospital
   B. the post office
   C. the gas station

6. A. the restaurant
   B. the library
   C. the police station

ANSWER SHEET			
1	A	B	C
2	A	B	C
3	A	B	C
4	A	B	C
5	A	B	C
6	A	B	C

2 Dictation 🎧

Listen and write the words you hear.

1. A: Excuse me. *Where's the* _____ ?
   B: It's on Front Street.

2. A: Excuse me. _____ near here?
   B: Yes, there is. It's in front of the library.

3. A: _____ of New Mexico?
   B: I'm not sure.

32

3 Conversation Check: Pair Work

Student A: Go to page 164.

Student B: Ask your partner the 2 questions below. Mark the places on the map.

1. Where's the post office?
2. Where's the bank?

How many questions did you ask your partner?	How many questions did you answer?
☐ 1 ☐ 2	☐ 1 ☐ 2

✔ LEARNING LOG

I know these words:

- ☐ across from
- ☐ ambulance
- ☐ ATM
- ☐ audiobook
- ☐ bank
- ☐ between
- ☐ bookmobile
- ☐ bus
- ☐ bus stop
- ☐ capital
- ☐ car
- ☐ checkout desk

- ☐ children's book
- ☐ community center
- ☐ crosswalk
- ☐ drugstore
- ☐ east
- ☐ enter
- ☐ equals
- ☐ fire station
- ☐ gas station
- ☐ hospital
- ☐ in back of
- ☐ in front of

- ☐ laundromat
- ☐ left
- ☐ less than
- ☐ librarian
- ☐ library
- ☐ library card
- ☐ magazine
- ☐ mailbox
- ☐ minus
- ☐ more than
- ☐ movie theater
- ☐ near

- ☐ next to
- ☐ north
- ☐ on the corner of
- ☐ one way
- ☐ park
- ☐ parking lot
- ☐ pay phone
- ☐ plus
- ☐ police station
- ☐ post office
- ☐ restaurant
- ☐ right

- ☐ school
- ☐ sidewalk
- ☐ south
- ☐ stop
- ☐ stoplight
- ☐ supermarket
- ☐ taxi
- ☐ truck
- ☐ turn
- ☐ video
- ☐ west

I can ask:

- ☐ Where's the post office?
- ☐ Is there a restaurant near here?
- ☐ Excuse me?

I can say:

- ☐ The library is next to the police station.
- ☐ There's a supermarket on Pine Street.
- ☐ There are five movie theaters near here.
- ☐ 5 + 3 = 8

I can write:

- ☐ an application for a library card

Spotlight: Writing

1 Read stories A and B below. Find these words.

Find the words with C.
c _a_ _r_ _o_ _l_
C __ __ __ __ __ __ __ __
c __ __
c __ __ __

Find the words with R.
r _e_ _a_ _d_
R __ __ __
r __ __ __ __
r __ __ __

STORIES 🎧

A.

Hi! My name is Carol. I'm from Colorado. I like to read, talk on the telephone, and go to the movies. I don't like to watch TV.

B.

My name is David. I'm from Reno, Nevada. I like to drive my car, listen to the radio, and go to parties. I don't like to clean my room.

2 Correct the story. Add 5 punctuation marks.

My name is Ann I like to watch

TV read books and go to school I don't

like to go to the supermarket

FOCUS ON WRITING: Punctuation Marks

- Use a period (.) at the end of a sentence.
  Example: He's a doctor.

- Use a comma (,) between words in a series.
  Example: I like to read, go to the library, and go to the park.

3 Complete the chart about you. Use the words below. Then add 3 more activities.

dance

I like to	I don't like to
dance	

go to the dentist

relax

eat

wash dishes

4 Write your own story.

My name is _____

_____

_____

_____

_____

Add your picture here.

What time is it?

THINGS TO DO

1 Learn Numbers 🎧

Listen to the numbers. Then listen and repeat.

12 twelve	13 thirteen	14 fourteen	15 fifteen	16 sixteen
17 seventeen	18 eighteen	19 nineteen	20 twenty	21 twenty-one
30 thirty	31 thirty-one	35 thirty-five	40 forty	50 fifty

2 Learn New Words 🎧

Look at the pictures. Listen to the words. Then listen and repeat.

TIMES
1. six o'clock
2. noon
3. midnight
4. 9:00 A.M.
5. 9:00 P.M.

TIME OF DAY
6. in the morning
7. in the afternoon
8. in the evening
9. at night

OTHER WORDS
10. before
11. after
12. minutes

Write the words under the pictures.

3 Practice the Conversation 🎧

Listen to the conversation. Then listen and repeat.

A: Excuse me. What time is it?

B: It's two o'clock .

A: Two o'clock ?

B: That's right.

Practice the conversation with a partner. Use the clocks below.

1. It's ___six o'clock___. (6:00 A.M.)

5. It's _____.

9. It's eleven forty-five

_____.

36

② It's _____ . (12:00 P.M.)

③ It's _____ . (12:00 A.M.)

④ It's _____ .

⑥ It's 8 o'clock _____ .

_____ .

⑦ It's two-fifteen _____

_____ .

⑧ It's seven-thirty_____

_____ .

⑩ It's ten _____ three.

⑪ It's ten _____ three.

⑫ It's fifteen _____ after four.

WINDOW ON GRAMMAR
Yes/No Questions with Be

A Read the questions and answers.

QUESTIONS	ANSWERS
Is the post office open at 9:00 A.M.?	Yes, **it is**.
Is your school open at 11:00 P.M.?	No, **it isn't**.
Are supermarket**s** open at night?	Yes, **they are**.
Are librarie**s** open at 3:00 A.M.?	No, **they aren't**.

B Complete the questions with *is* or *are*. Then ask a partner.

1. _____ your school open at night?

2. _____ gas stations open at midnight?

3. _____ the post office open at noon?

4. _____ restaurants open at 6:00 P.M.?

5. _____ banks open after 9:00 P.M.?

2 LESSON

Is the library open on Monday?

THINGS TO DO

1 Talk About the Picture

Write 5 things about the picture.

EXAMPLE: There are people in front of the library.

Share your ideas with the class.

2 Learn New Words

Listen and repeat the words.

①　Sunday　　　⑤　Thursday　　　⑧　No smoking.
②　Monday　　　⑥　Friday　　　　⑨　No eating.
③　Tuesday　　　⑦　Saturday
④　Wednesday

Find the words and signs in the picture.

3 Practice the Conversation

Listen to the conversation. Then listen and repeat.

A: Is the library open on Monday?
B: Yes, it's open from noon to 9:00.
A: From noon to 9:00?
B: Right.

Closed =
Not Open

Practice the conversation with a partner. Use these items.

1 Tuesday	2 Wednesday	3 Saturday	4
10 A.M. to 9 P.M.	noon to 9 P.M.	10 A.M. to 5 P.M.	

★★★★★★★★★★★★★★★★★★★★★★★★★★★★★★★★★★★★★

 TRY THIS　Write the hours of your library or school.

EXAMPLE: Sunday　　9:00 A.M. to 5:00 P.M.
　　　　　Monday　　9:00 A.M. to 7:00 P.M.

★★★★★★★★★★★★★★★★★★★★★★★★★★★★★★★★★★★★★

3 LESSON

It's five cents.

Coins

① a _____penny_____
(one cent/1¢)

② a _____
(five cents/5¢)

③ a _____
(ten cents/10¢)

④ a _____
(twenty-five cents/25¢)

⑤ a _____
(fifty cents/50¢)

THINGS TO DO

1 Learn New Words 🎧

Look at the pictures. Listen to the words. Then listen and repeat.

① penny   ⑤ half-dollar   ⑨ twenty dollars
② nickel   ⑥ dollar   ⑩ fifty dollars
③ dime   ⑦ five dollars   ⑪ one hundred dollars
④ quarter   ⑧ ten dollars   ⑫ one thousand dollars

Write the words under the pictures.

2 Write

Add the coins.

1. ___thirty-five cents (35¢)___   2. _____

3. _____   4. _____

3 Practice the Conversation 🎧

Listen to the conversation. Then listen and repeat.

A: How much is it?

B: Thirty cents .

A: Are you sure?

B: Yes.

Practice the conversation with a partner. Ask about the 4 items in Activity 2.

Bills

⑥ a _____
($1.00)

⑦ _____
($5.00)

⑧ _____
($10.00)

⑨ _____
($20.00)

⑩ _____
($50.00)

⑪ _____
($100.00)

⑫ _____
($1,000.00)

WINDOW ON GRAMMAR
Questions with *How much*

⭐ **A** Read the questions and answers.

QUESTIONS	ANSWERS
How much is it?	It's fifty cents.
How much is the pen?	It's one dollar.
How much is a late book?	It's five cents a day.

⭐ **B** Work with a partner. Ask and answer 5 questions.

How much is	a penny a nickel a dime a quarter a dollar _____	and	a penny? a nickel? a dime? a quarter? a dollar? _____?

EXAMPLE: A: How much is a penny and a quarter?
B: It's twenty-six cents (26¢).

41

4 LESSON

Checks

THINGS TO DO

1 Learn New Words

Look at the pictures. Listen to the words. Then listen and repeat.

① check   ② check number   ③ amount   ④ signature

2 Read

Complete this chart with information from the 3 checks.

Check #	To	Amount	For
124	Coral Beach Library	$12.00	late books
125			

3 Write

Write the check amounts.

1. $25.00   _Twenty-five and_ ^{00}/100 _dollars_

2. $31.50   _____

3. $56.34   _____

Write a check to Ace Drugstore for $53.10.

★ ★

TRY THIS Draw a check. Then write a check for something you want.

★ ★

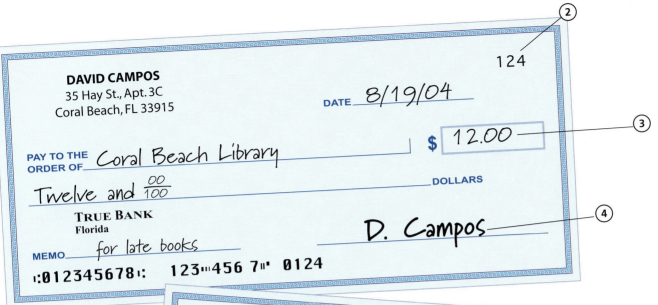

② 124

DAVID CAMPOS
35 Hay St., Apt. 3C
Coral Beach, FL 33915

DATE 8/19/04

③ $ 12.00

PAY TO THE
ORDER OF Coral Beach Library

Twelve and $\frac{00}{100}$ ——————— DOLLARS

TRUE BANK
Florida

④ D. Campos

MEMO for late books

⑆012345678⑆ 123ⅲ456 7ⅱ 0124

DAVID CAMPOS
35 Hay St., Apt. 3C
Coral Beach, FL 33915

125

DATE 8/23/04

PAY TO THE
ORDER OF CASH

Fifty and $\frac{00}{100}$

$ 50.00

TRUE BANK
Florida ——————— DOLLARS

MEMO for food

D. Campos

⑆012345678⑆ 123ⅲ456 7ⅱ 0125

126

DATE 8/27/04

st Office $ 18.50

——————— DOLLARS

D. Campos

26

WINDOW ON MATH
Adding and Subtracting

A Listen to the sentences. Then listen and repeat. 🎧

10¢ + 25¢ = 35¢	$1.00 + .50 = $1.50
50¢ + 25¢ = 75¢	$5.00 + $2.00 = $7.00
5¢ – 1¢ = 4¢	$10.00 – $1.00 = $9.00
60¢ – 10¢ = 50¢	$50.00 – $30.00 = $20.00

B Write the missing numbers. Read the sentences to a partner.

1. $3.00 – $1.50 = _____
2. $.75 – $.25 = _____
3. 50¢ + 10¢ = _____
4. $10.00 + $12.00 = _____
5. $5.00 + $10.00 = _____
6. $20.00 + $1.50 = _____
7. $100.00 – $20.00 = _____
8. $100.00 + $50.00 = _____

43

5 LESSON

Thank you for calling.

1 Practice the Conversation: Asking about Business Hours 🎧

Listen to the conversation. Then listen and repeat.

A: Hello. Anderson's Drugstore. Can I help you?

B: Yes. What are your hours on Thursday ?

A: We're open from 8:00 to 6:00 .

B: Thank you.

Practice the conversation with a partner. Use these items.

1 Saturday
from 9:00 to noon

2 Sunday
from noon to 7:00

3 Tuesday
from 9:00 to 9:00

4 Wednesday
from 9:00 to 9:00

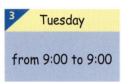
5

2 Practice the Conversation: Calling Directory Assistance 🎧

Listen to the conversation. Then listen and repeat.

A: Welcome to Horizon. What city and state?

B: Miami, Florida .

A: What listing?

B: Rafael Hernandez .

A: The number is area code 305-555-5938 .

Practice the conversation with a partner. Use these items.

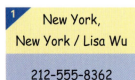
1 New York, New York / Lisa Wu
212-555-8362

2 Houston, Texas / Rita Smith
713-555-9146

3 Santa Ana, California /Grace Chan
714-555-2020

4 Miami, Florida / Shirley Garcia
305-555-7864

5

3 Listen and Write: Listening to a Recorded Message

Listen and write the missing numbers. Then listen and check.

Thank you for calling the Coral Beach Public Library. For hours, press 1.

The library is open Monday through Thursday

from _____11:00_____ to _____ .

On Friday and Saturday, the library is open

from _____ to _____ .

Good-bye.

WINDOW ON PRONUNCIATION
Thirteen or *Thirty*? Syllable Stress in Numbers

A Listen to the words. Then listen and repeat.

thirteen (13)	thirty (30)
fourteen (14)	forty (40)
fifteen (15)	fifty (50)
sixteen (16)	sixty (60)
seventeen (17)	seventy (70)
eighteen (18)	eighty (80)
nineteen (19)	ninety (90)

B Listen and circle the numbers you hear.

1. 13   30   5. 17   70

2. 14   40   6. 18   80

3. 15   50   7. 19   90

4. 16   60

C Listen and point to the numbers you hear.

1. It's **six-fifty / six-fifteen**.

2. It's **fifteen / fifty** cents.

3. From **9:30 / 9:13** A.M. to 6:00 P.M.

4. The price is **$3.18 / $3.80**.

Listen as your partner says the numbers. Circle the numbers you hear.

UNIT 3: Time and Money

Business Hours

1 Read

Read the store signs. Answer the questions below.

WESTMINSTER BANK

Monday	9:00 a.m.–3:00 p.m.
Tuesday	9:00 a.m.–3:00 p.m.
Wednesday	9:00 a.m.–3:00 p.m.
Thursday	9:00 a.m.–3:00 p.m.
Friday	9:00 a.m.–3:00 p.m.
Saturday	**closed**
Sunday	**closed**

Johnson's Drugstore

Monday	7:30 a.m.–8:30 p.m.
Tuesday	7:30 a.m.–8:30 p.m.
Wednesday	7:30 a.m.–8:30 p.m.
Thursday	7:30 a.m.–8:30 p.m.
Friday	7:30 a.m.–8:30 p.m.
Saturday	8:30 a.m.–6:30 p.m.
Sunday	8:30 a.m.–6:30 p.m.

U.S. Post Office
Hours of Operation

Monday:	9–4
Tuesday:	9–4
Wednesday:	9–4
Thursday:	9–4
Friday:	9–4
Saturday:	9–2
Sunday:	Closed

ARMITAGE HOSPITAL VISITING HOURS

Open seven days a week.

Monday, Tuesday, Wednesday, Thursday, Friday, Saturday, Sunday

10 a.m.–12 p.m. & 7 p.m.–9 p.m.

1. What's open on Sunday morning? _The drugstore and the hospital are._ _____

2. When are both the bank and the post office open? _____

3. What's open every day? _____

4. What is closed on Sunday? _____

5. When's the post office open on Saturday? _____

6. It's 8:00 P.M. on Monday. What's open? _____

7. It's noon on Sunday. Is the bank open? _____

2 How Much Is It?

Study the pictures. Answer the questions.

1. How much is a telephone call? _____35¢_____

2. How much is it for two hours? _____

    How much is it for three hours? _____

3. How much is it for two hours? _____

    How much is it for three hours? _____

4. How much are two loads? _____

    How much are three loads? _____

3 Write

Find information about 3 places in your town. Then report to the class.

NAME	ADDRESS	TELEPHONE NUMBER	HOURS
State St. Bank	224 State Street	603–555–4873	Monday–Friday 9:00 – 4:00

7 LESSON

What do you know?

1 Listening Review 🎧

Listen and choose the time you hear. Use the Answer Sheet.

1.
   A   B   C

2.
   A   B   C

3.
   A   B   C

4.
   A   B   C

ANSWER SHEET			
1	A	B	C
2	A	B	C
3	A	B	C
4	A	B	C
5	A	B	C
6	A	B	C
7	A	B	C
8	A	B	C
9	A	B	C
10	A	B	C

Listen and choose the correct answer. Use the Answer Sheet.

5. A. 10:00 A.M.
   B. 9:00 to 5:00
   C. nine o'clock

6. A. It's nine o'clock.
   B. It's Friday.
   C. It's a quarter.

7. A. It's 1:00 A.M.
   B. It's ten cents.
   C. It's the library.

8. A. at 7:00
   B. $7.00
   C. at school

9. A. Yes, it is.
   B. on Monday
   C. Tuesday

10. A. three hundred dollars
    B. from 8:00 to 6:00
    C. at the library

2 Conversation Check: Pair Work

Student A: Go to page 165.

Student B: Ask your partner questions to complete this chart.

EXAMPLE: **B:** When is the community center open on Tuesday?

A: From noon to 8 P.M.

	Sunday	Monday	Tuesday	Wednesday	Thursday	Friday	Saturday
Community Center	closed	closed	noon to 8 P.M.	noon to 8 P.M.	noon to 8 P.M.	noon to 10 P.M.	
Laundromat	7 A.M. to 10 P.M.	noon to 10 P.M.	noon to 10 P.M.	10 A.M. to 10 P.M.	10 A.M. to 10 P.M.	10 A.M. to 10 P.M.	
Drugstore		8 A.M. to 9 P.M.	8 A.M. to 9 P.M.	8 A.M. to 9 P.M.	8 A.M. to 9 P.M.	8 A.M. to 9 P.M.	8 A.M. to 6 P.M.
Supermarket	8 A.M. to 8 P.M.	6 A.M. to midnight	6 A.M. to midnight	6 A.M. to midnight	6 A.M. to midnight		6 A.M. to 10 P.M.

✔

How many questions did you ask your partner?	How many questions did you answer?
☐ 1 ☐ 2 ☐ 3 ☐ 4 ☐ 5	☐ 1 ☐ 2 ☐ 3 ☐ 4 ☐ 5

✔ LEARNING LOG

I know these words:

☐ after	☐ dime	☐ half-dollar	☐ noon	☐ signature	☐ Tuesday
☐ afternoon	☐ dollar	☐ hours	☐ o'clock	☐ sixteen	☐ twelve
☐ A.M.	☐ eighteen	☐ midnight	☐ open	☐ sixty	☐ twenty
☐ amount	☐ eighty	☐ minute	☐ penny	☐ smoking	☐ twenty–one
☐ before	☐ evening	☐ Monday	☐ personal check	☐ Sunday	☐ Wednesday
☐ cents	☐ fifteen	☐ morning	☐ P.M.	☐ thirteen	☐ week
☐ check	☐ fifty	☐ nickel	☐ quarter	☐ thirty	
☐ check number	☐ forty	☐ night	☐ Saturday	☐ thirty–five	
☐ closed	☐ fourteen	☐ nineteen	☐ seventeen	☐ thirty–one	
☐ day	☐ Friday	☐ ninety	☐ seventy	☐ Thursday	

I can ask:

- ☐ What time is it?
- ☐ Is the library open on Sunday?
- ☐ What are your hours?
- ☐ How much is it?
- ☐ Are you sure?

I can say:

- ☐ It's two o'clock.
- ☐ That's right.
- ☐ It's open from noon to 9.
- ☐ It's fifty cents.

I can write:

- ☐ numbers 12 to 90
- ☐ a personal check
- ☐ amounts of money

49

Spotlight: Grammar

YES/NO QUESTIONS AND ANSWERS WITH BE

I	you, they	he, she, it
Am I on State Street? Yes, **you are**. No, **you aren't** No, **you're not**.	**Are you** from Mexico? Yes, **I am**. No, **I am not**. No, **I'm not**. **Are you and Tina** from Canada? Yes, **we are**. No, **we aren't**. No, **we're not**. **Are the students** in class? Yes, **they are**. No, **they aren't**. No, **they're not**.	**Is Bob** a teacher? Yes, **he is**. No, **he isn't**. No, **he's not**. **Is Tina** a student? Yes, **she is**. No, **she isn't**. No, **she's not**. **Is your book** from China? Yes, **it is**. No, **it isn't**. No, **it's not**.

1 Write the words in the correct order. Then answer the questions.

1. A: *Are you from Mexico?* _____ (you / from / Mexico / Are / ?)

   B: _____

2. A: _____ (your school / near a restaurant / Is / ?)

   B: _____

3. A: _____ (in the morning / Is / your class / ?)

   B: _____

4. A: _____ (five dollars / ten dollars / more than / Is / ?)

   B: _____

5. A: _____ (Are / your class / Don and Daisy / in / ?)

   B: _____

2 Complete the conversations. Then practice with a partner.

1. A: ____*Is*____ your signature on the check?

   B: Yes, it _____.

2. A: _____ the library open in the evening?

   B: Yes, it _____.

3. A: _____ the bank on State Street?

   B: No, it _____.

4. A: _____ I near the bank?

   B: Yes, you _____.

INFORMATION QUESTIONS WITH *BE*

What	is	your name?	What	are	your hours?	*Contractions*
Where	is	the supermarket?	Where	are	your books?	What's
When	is	the next holiday?	When	are	banks open?	Where's
Who	is	your teacher?	Who	are	Mutt and Jeff?	When's
How much	is	one notebook?	How much	are	the notebooks?	Who's

3 Match the questions and answers.

1. _e_ What is on your chair?

2. ___ Who is your doctor?

3. ___ When is the post office closed?

4. ___ How much is a notebook?

5. ___ Who are Bob, John, and Tina?

6. ___ Where are the videos?

7. ___ How much are the magazines?

a. They are my classmates.

b. It's about $3.00.

c. They're on my desk.

d. Dr. Baldwin

e. my book and my notebook

f. on Sunday

g. They are $5.00.

4 Complete the conversations. Then practice with a partner.

1. A: ____*When's*____ the post office open on Saturday?

   B: It's open from 9 to noon.

2. A: _____ the man on the one dollar bill?

   B: He's George Washington.

3. A: _____ the chairs?

   B: They're in Room 102.

4. A: _____ the bus stop?

   B: It's across the street.

5. A: _____ ten plus ten?

   B: It's twenty.

6. A: _____ the U.S. President?

   B: _____.

When is your birthday?

LESSON 1

① _____ ② _____

1 Learn New Words 🎧

Look at the pictures. Listen to the words. Then listen and repeat.

① January	⑦ July	⑬ cold
② February	⑧ August	⑭ warm
③ March	⑨ September	⑮ hot
④ April	⑩ October	⑯ rainy
⑤ May	⑪ November	⑰ sunny
⑥ June	⑫ December	⑱ cloudy

Write the words under the pictures.

⑦ _____ ⑧ _____

Weather Words

2 Write

Complete the sentences. Then read your sentences to a partner.

1. We are now in the month of _____.
2. It's hot here in _____.
3. It's cold here in _____.
4. It's rainy here in _____.
5. My birthday is in _____.
6. My favorite month is _____.
7. Next month is _____.

⑬ _____

3 Interview

Interview 5 classmates. Write their answers in a chart like this.

> EXAMPLE: A: When is your birthday?
>   B: It's in September.

⑮ _____

NAME	WHEN IS YOUR BIRTHDAY?
Mei	September

How many birthdays are in each month?

⑰ _____

Months of the Year

3. _____

4. _____

5. _____

6. _____

9. _____

10. _____

11. _____

12. _____

14. _____

16. _____

18. _____

WINDOW ON GRAMMAR
Questions with *How many*

A Read the questions.

How many month**s** are in a year?
How many week**s** are in a year?
How many day**s** are in a year?

B Complete the questions. (Many answers are possible.) Then ask a partner.

months   weeks   days   hours   minutes

1. How many _____ are in a week?

2. How many _____ are in a day?

3. How many _____ are in an hour?

4. How many _____ are in February?

5. How many _____ are in August?

The party is on Sunday.

THINGS TO DO

1 Learn Ordinal Numbers 🎧

Listen to the numbers. Then listen and repeat.

1st first	2nd second	3rd third	4th fourth
5th fifth	6th sixth	7th seventh	8th eighth
9th ninth	10th tenth	11th eleventh	12th twelfth
13th thirteenth	14th fourteenth	15th fifteenth	16th sixteenth

2 Learn New Words 🎧

Look at the pictures. Listen to the words. Then listen and repeat.

① doctor's appointment ④ PTO meeting ⑥ basketball game
② computer class ⑤ job interview ⑦ dentist's appointment
③ birthday party

Work with a partner. Ask about Alice. Ask about each picture.

A: When is Alice's doctor's appointment ?
B: It's on May first .
A: What day is that?
B: Tuesday .

3 Practice the Conversation 🎧

Listen to the conversation. Then listen and repeat.

A: Alice, do you want to meet on the first ?
B: What day is that?
A: Tuesday .
B: Oh, sorry. I have a doctor's appointment on the first .

Practice the conversation with a partner. Ask about these dates.

 1 third   **2** sixth   **3** eighth   **4** ninth   **5**

Sunday	Mon

MAY

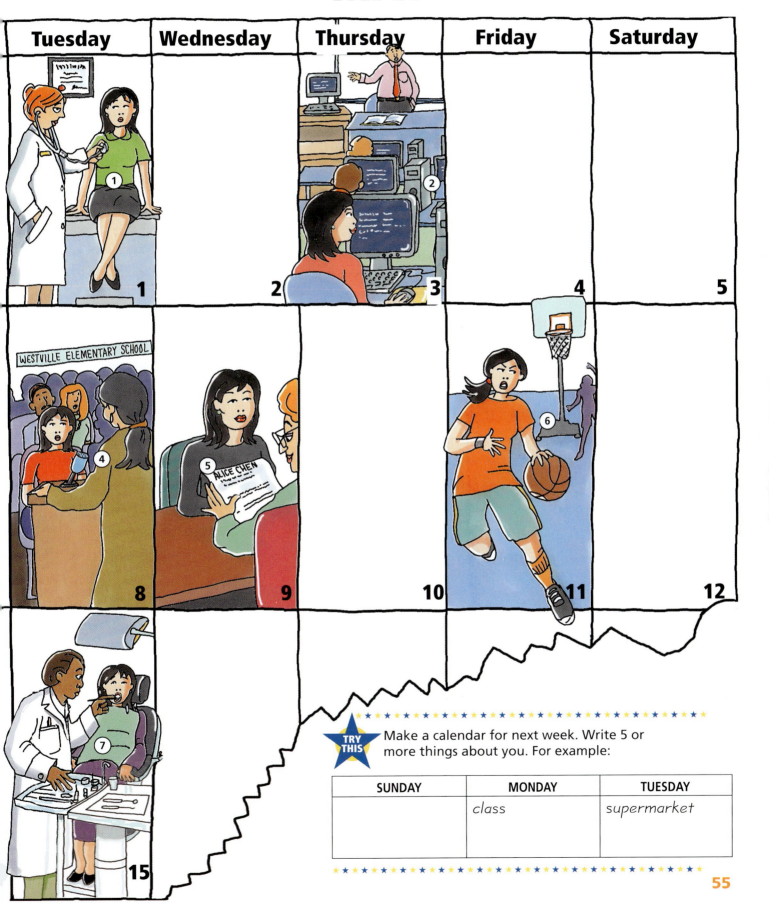

Tuesday	Wednesday	Thursday	Friday	Saturday

TRY THIS ★ Make a calendar for next week. Write 5 or more things about you. For example:

SUNDAY	MONDAY	TUESDAY
	class	supermarket

55

3 LESSON

What's the date?

THINGS TO DO

1 Learn Ordinal Numbers 🎧

Listen to the numbers. Then listen and repeat.

17th seventeenth	18th eighteenth	19th nineteenth	20th twentieth
21st twenty-first	22nd twenty-second	23rd twenty-third	24th twenty-fourth
25th twenty-fifth	26th twenty-sixth	27th twenty-seventh	28th twenty-eighth

2 Write

Complete the chart. Use the appointment cards and calendar.

Name	Date	Time	Day
Henry	June 22	10 A.M.	Friday
Sue			
Nancy			
Alice			
Sam			

3 Practice the Conversation 🎧

Listen to the conversation. Then listen and repeat.

A: When's Henry's appointment?

B: It's on June twenty-second .

A: What time?

B: At 10:00 A.M.

A: What day is that?

B: Friday .

Practice the conversation with a partner. Ask about these people.

 Sue's   Nancy's   Alice's   Paul's   Lisa's

Sue Chen

has an appointment on

(M) TU W TH F

June 18 @ 4 p.m.

Please call to cancel.

Henry Chen

HAS AN APPOINTMENT ON

June 22 AT 10 a.m.

If Unable To Keep Appointment Kindly Give 24 Hours No

 Randolph Optometry
Next appointment for:
Lisa Chen

Date: June 20   Time: 4 p.m.

Mon.   Tues.   (Wed.)
Thurs.   Fri.

**DENTAL ASSOCIATES
OF CENTRAL NEW YORK**

Appointment Card

For: Chris Chen

On: June 25

At: 9 a.m.

M ✓
T ___
W ___
TH ___
F ___

If unable to keep this appointment,
kindly give 24 hours notice.

Nancy Chen
has an appointment on
June 27 @ 12 p.m.

M   TU   ⓦ   TH   F

*Please kindly give us 24 hours notice if you will
need to cancel your appointment. Thank you!*

Appointment Card

Alice Chen
June 28 @ 11 a.m.

Mon.   Tues.   Wed.   Ⓣhurs.   Fri.

Name: Sam Chen

Your next appointment is on:

June 21 at 9 a.m.

We reserve the right to charge for appointments canceled
or broken without 24 hours advance notice.

Name: Paul Chen

Your next appointment is on:

June 19 at 9 a.m.

Mon.   T̲u̲e̲s̲.̲   Wed.   Thurs.   Fri.

JUNE

SUN	MON	TUE	WED	THU	FRI	SAT
					1	2
3	4	5	6	7	8	9
10	11	12	13	14	15	16
17	18	19	20	21	22	23
24	25	26	27	28	29	30

WINDOW ON MATH
Writing Dates

 A Read these dates.

> 12/25/02 = December 25, 2002
> 1/1/95 = January 1, 1995
> 8/19/03 = August 19, 2003

 B Write the dates another way.

3/16/80 = _____   April 11, 1944 = _____

5/19/01 = _____   February 17, 2002 = _____

 C What's the date today? Write it 2 ways.

_____   _____

57

4 LESSON

Holidays

THINGS TO DO

1 Read 🎧

Read about 6 holidays in the United States. Take notes in the chart. Share your answers with a partner.

NAME OF HOLIDAY	WHEN?
1. New Year's Day	January 1
2.	
3.	
4.	
5.	
6.	

2 Write

Answer the questions.

WHAT'S YOUR FAVORITE HOLIDAY?	WHEN IS IT?

3 Interview

Ask 5 classmates about their favorite holidays. Make a chart like this. Write their answers.

A: What's your favorite holiday?

B: New Year's Day .

A: When is it?

B: In January .

NAME	HOLIDAY	MONTH
Jaime	New Year's Day	January

For people in the United States, New Year's Day is on January 1. That's the first day of the new year.

Election Day in the United States is on the first Tuesday after the first Monday in November.

2

Valentine's Day is on February 14.

3

In the United States, Independence Day is on the fourth of July.

4

Labor Day is on the first Monday in September. This holiday is for workers in the United States.

6

Thanksgiving is a big holiday in the United States. It's on the fourth Thursday in November.

WINDOW ON GRAMMAR
Singular and Plural Nouns

A Read the words.

SINGULAR		PLURAL	SINGULAR		PLURAL
holid**ay**	–	holiday**s**	fami**ly**	–	famil**ies**
ban**k**	–	bank**s**	libra**ry**	–	librar**ies**
mon**th**	–	month**s**	count**ry**	–	countr**ies**
minut**e**	–	minute**s**	par**ty**	–	part**ies**

B Write the missing singular or plural form.

one family / two _____

one school / two _____

one city / two _____

one _____ / two states

one _____ / two hours

one _____ / two post offices

LESSON 5

I need to cancel my appointment.

1 Practice the Conversation: Making an Appointment

Listen to the conversation. Then listen and repeat.

A: Dr. Lambert's office.

B: Yes, this is Jim Brown . I'd like to make an appointment.

A: Okay. Our next opening is on March 6th at 11:00 .

B: Great. I'll take it.

Practice the conversation with a partner.
Use these items.

1 Gina Mata	2 Ken Park	3 Tom Lin	4 Alice Lopez	5
March 10th at 2:00	March 22nd at 4:00	April 12th at 10:30	April 13th at 11:45	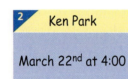

2 Practice the Conversation: Canceling an Appointment

Listen to the conversation. Then listen and repeat.

A: Dr. Lambert's office.

B: This is Jim Brown . I need to cancel my appointment.

A: When is it?

B: It's on March 6th at 11:00 .

A: Okay. Thanks for calling.

Practice the conversation with a partner.
Use these items.

1 Gina Mata / March 10th at 2:00	2 Ken Park / March 22nd at 4:00	3 Tom Lin / April 12th at 10:30	4 Alice Lopez / April 13th at 11:45	5

3 Practice the Conversation: Rescheduling an Appointment 🎧

Listen to the conversation. Then listen and repeat.

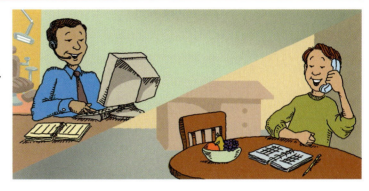

A: Dr. Lambert's office.

B: This is Jim Brown . I need to reschedule my appointment.

A: Okay. I have an opening on May 5ᵗʰ at 2:00 .

B: That's good. Thank you.

Practice the conversation with a partner.
Use these items.

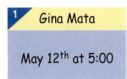
1 Gina Mata
May 12ᵗʰ at 5:00

2 Ken Park
May 16ᵗʰ at 3:00

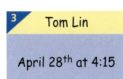
3 Tom Lin
April 28ᵗʰ at 4:15

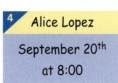
4 Alice Lopez
September 20ᵗʰ at 8:00

5

WINDOW ON PRONUNCIATION 🎧
Short *A* and Long *A*

 A Listen to the words. Then listen and repeat.

1. male	5. make	9. map	13. raise	17. state
2. gas	6. magazine	10. back	14. after	18. day
3. date	7. basketball	11. May	15. table	19. April
4. that	8. cashier	12. rainy	16. okay	20. sale

Write the words in the correct place.

Sounds like letter *A* (long *A*)	Sounds like *a* in map (short *A*)
male, date	*gas, that*

 B Work with a partner. Ask and answer the questions.

1. Is Texas a city or a state?
2. What date is today?
3. What month is after April?
4. What days of the week is your class?
5. Is Saturday before or after Friday?

School Calendars

1 Read

Read the school calendar. Answer the questions below.

SOUTH BEACH CITY PUBLIC SCHOOLS

First Semester

September 2 (Mon.)	Labor Day (Holiday – Schools Closed)
September 3 (Tues.)	First Day of School
October 4 (Fri.)	Progress Reports Issued
November 11 (Mon.)	Veterans' Day (Holiday – Schools Closed)
November 12 (Tues.)	Progress Reports Issued
November 28 and 29 (Thurs., Fri.)	Thanksgiving (Holiday – Schools Closed)
December 11 (Wed.)	Report Cards Issued
December 23 – January 1	Winter Holidays (Schools Closed)

PROGRESS REPORT

SOUTH BEACH CITY JR. HIGH SCHOOL

Student Name: Dita Warner
Student ID: 6072

Grade: 07
Year: 2004-05

Course	Number	Teacher	Term 1	Term 2
English	112	Gallo, F	S	S
World Civics	211	Truncelino, E	N	S
Earth Science	311	Bennet, H	S	S
Geometry	421	Tedone, A	S	S
German	622	Gebhart, E	N	N
	350	Langdon, J	S	S

REPORT CARD

SOUTH BEACH CITY JR. HIGH SCHOOL

Student Name: Brian Teese
Student ID: 7470

Grade: 07
Year: 2004-05

Course	Number	Teacher	Term 1	Term 2
English	112	Mearek, S	98	97
World Civics	211	Colman, D	82	86
Earth Science	311	Bennet, H	83	89
Geometry	421	Tambrey, J	95	94
Italian	722	Fabriano, C	72	81
Phys Ed	350	Langdon, J	93	95

Absences: 3
Tardy: 0

1. When is the first day of school in South Beach?

_____

2. What holiday is in September?

_____

3. When are the schools closed in November?

_____

4. How many holidays are there between September 1 and December 1?

_____

5. When are Progress Reports issued?

_____

6. When do you think school opens after the Winter Holidays?

_____

2 Mark the Calendar

Write the South Beach school events and holidays on the calendar for November.

NOVEMBER

SUN	MON	TUE	WED	THU	FRI	SAT
					1	2
3	4	5	6	7	8	9
10	11	12 *Progress Reports issued*	13	14	15	16
17	18	19	20	21	22	23
24	25	26	27	28	29	30

3 Write

Make a calendar for next month. Write the name of the month. Write the dates.
Write important events on your calendar.

Month : _____

SUN	MON	TUE	WED	THU	FRI	SAT

LESSON 7

What do you know?

1 Listening Review 🎧

Listen and choose the word you hear. Use the Answer Sheet.

1. A. country   B. countries
2. A. month   B. months
3. A. holiday   B. holidays
4. A. family   B. families

5. A. dollar   B. dollars
6. A. cent   B. cents
7. A. state   B. states
8. A. city   B. cities

Listen and choose the best answer. Use the Answer Sheet.

9. A. on Monday
   B. at 5
   C. 7

10. A. twelve
    B. January
    C. December

11. A. February
    B. the eighth
    C. Monday

12. A. Sunday
    B. Tuesday
    C. Thursday

13. A. August
    B. October
    C. November

14. A. in Mexico
    B. in November
    C. in the city

ANSWER SHEET

1	A	B	
2	A	B	
3	A	B	
4	A	B	
5	A	B	
6	A	B	
7	A	B	
8	A	B	
9	A	B	C
10	A	B	C
11	A	B	C
12	A	B	C
13	A	B	C
14	A	B	C
15	A	B	C
16	A	B	C

Listen and choose the correct appointment card. Use the Answer Sheet.

15.

_____ Henry _____
Next appointment:
M   TU   W   TH   (F)
April 2   at   3 p.m.
Please call 24 hours in advance to cancel.

A.

Appointment
_____ Paul _____
April 12 @   3 p.m.
☐ Mon. ☐ Tues. ☑ Wed. ☐ Thurs. ☐ Fri.

B.

_____ Jon's _____
appointment
April 22   at   3 p.m.
MON   TUE   WED   (THU)   FRI   SAT

C.

16.

_____ Nancy Chen _____
has an appointment on
Friday, June 22
@   12 p.m.
*Please kindly give us 24 hours notice if you will
need to cancel your appointment. Thank you!*

A.

Name: _____ Sam _____
Your next appointment is on:
_____ Monday, May 19 _____
at   9 a.m.
If Unable To Keep Appointment Kindly Give 24 Hours Notice.

B.

APPOINTMENT
_____ Sue _____
June 20   at   2 p.m.
☐ MON. ☐ TUES. ☑ WED. ☐ THURS. ☐ FRI.

C.

2 Conversation Check: Pair Work

Student A: Go to page 165.
Student B: Ask your partner questions about appointment cards 1 and 2. Answer questions about cards 3 and 4.

EXAMPLE: **B:** When is John's appointment?
A: It's on March 9.
B: What time?

1

John

Has an appointment on:

March 9 at _____

Mon.   Tues.   Wed.   Thurs.   Fri.

3
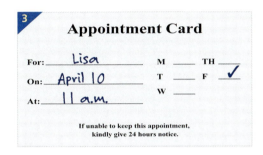

Appointment Card

For: Lisa   M ____   TH ____
On: April 10   T ____   F ✓
At: 11 a.m.   W ____

*If unable to keep this appointment,
kindly give 24 hours notice.*

2 Name: Sue

Your next appointment is on:

_____ at _____

*We reserve the right to charge for appointments canceled
or broken without 24 hours advance notice.*

4
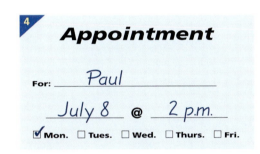

Appointment

For: ____ Paul ____

July 8 @ 2 p.m.

☑ **Mon.** ☐ **Tues.** ☐ **Wed.** ☐ **Thurs.** ☐ **Fri.**

✓	How many questions did you ask your partner?	How many questions did you answer?
	☐ 1 ☐ 2 ☐ 3 ☐ 4 ☐ 5	☐ 1 ☐ 2 ☐ 3 ☐ 4 ☐ 5

✔ LEARNING LOG

I know these words:

- ☐ appointment
- ☐ April
- ☐ August
- ☐ basketball game
- ☐ birthday party
- ☐ cloudy
- ☐ cold
- ☐ December
- ☐ dentist's appointment
- ☐ doctor's appointment

- ☐ eighteenth
- ☐ eighth
- ☐ eleventh
- ☐ February
- ☐ fifteenth
- ☐ fifth
- ☐ first
- ☐ fourteenth
- ☐ fourth
- ☐ hot

- ☐ January
- ☐ job interview
- ☐ July
- ☐ June
- ☐ March
- ☐ May
- ☐ month
- ☐ nineteenth
- ☐ ninth
- ☐ November

- ☐ October
- ☐ PTO meeting
- ☐ rainy
- ☐ second
- ☐ September
- ☐ seventeenth
- ☐ seventh
- ☐ sixteenth
- ☐ sixth
- ☐ sunny

- ☐ tenth
- ☐ third
- ☐ thirteenth
- ☐ thirtieth
- ☐ twelfth
- ☐ twentieth
- ☐ warm
- ☐ weather

I can ask:

- ☐ When is your birthday?
- ☐ What day is that?
- ☐ When is your appointment?
- ☐ When is Labor Day?

I can say:

- ☐ It's on May first.
- ☐ I'd like to make an appointment.
- ☐ I need to cancel an appointment.
- ☐ I'd like to reschedule my appointment.

I can write:

- ☐ dates in two ways
- ☐ appointments on a calendar

Spotlight: Writing

1 Read stories A and B below. Find these words.

Find the singular nouns with these letters.

h <u>o</u> <u>l</u> <u>i</u> <u>d</u> <u>a</u> <u>y</u>

m __ __ __ __ __

f __ __ __ __ __

f __ __ __ __ __ __

c __ __ __ __ __ __

Find the plural nouns.

__ __ __ __ __ __ s

__ __ __ __ __ __ __ __ s

__ __ __ __ __ __ __ s

__ __ __ __ __ __ __ __ s

Stories 🎧

A.

My name in Ling. My favorite holiday is Chinese New Year. It's in January or February. I like this holiday because I get money from my mother and father. We go to see the parades. We watch the fireworks at night and eat a lot of food, too.

B.

My name is Eduardo. My favorite holiday is Christmas. It's in December. I like this holiday because I am with my family. We go to church. We go to parties and give presents.

2 Correct the punctuation. Add 10 capital letters.

my name is fatima. my favorite holiday is ramadan. this year it is in march. i like this holiday because i visit with my family. we go to egypt to see them.

3 Write your own story.

FOCUS ON WRITING: Capital Letters

Capitalize:

- the first word in a sentence.

  EXAMPLE: <u>H</u>e is a doctor.

- a person's first and last name.

  EXAMPLE: <u>J</u>ohn <u>S</u>mith

- the name of a country, state, or city.

  EXAMPLE: <u>M</u>exico, <u>C</u>alifornia, <u>L</u>os <u>A</u>ngeles

- the name of a language.

  EXAMPLE: <u>E</u>nglish, <u>S</u>panish, <u>C</u>hinese

- the days of the week.

  EXAMPLE: <u>M</u>onday

- the months of the year.

  EXAMPLE: <u>J</u>anuary

- the name of a holiday.

  EXAMPLE: <u>T</u>hanksgiving

- the pronoun *I*.

  EXAMPLE: This is where <u>I</u> live.

Add your picture here.

My name is _____.

_____

_____

_____

_____

_____

_____

_____

_____

_____

LESSON 1

Shirts, Skirts, and Sweaters

Clothes for M

THINGS TO DO

1 Learn New Words 🎧

Look at the pictures. Listen to the words. Then listen and repeat.

1. necktie
2. undershirt
3. briefs
4. shoes
5. boots
6. coat
7. shirt
8. sweater
9. hat
10. T-shirt
11. jacket
12. pajamas
13. socks
14. pants
15. shorts
16. blouse
17. skirt
18. dress

Write the words above the pictures.

2 Learn New Words 🎧

Look at the squares. Listen to the colors. Then listen and repeat.

blue	yellow	red	black
brown	green	purple	white

3 Practice the Conversation 🎧

Listen to the conversation. Then listen and repeat.

A: What color is the jacket ?

B: It's brown .

Practice the conversation with a partner. Use these items from the pictures.

1. coat
2. skirt
3. T-shirt
4. necktie
5. 💡

1 _____

6 _____

2 _____

10 _____

3 _____

TRY THIS
Choose 3 colors and make a chart. List 5 thir in your classroom for each color.

blue	white	yellow
Ann's sweater	Juan's shirt	my notebook

Clothes for Men and Women

Clothes for Women

④ _____

⑤ _____

⑯ _____

⑦ _____

⑧ _____

⑨ _____

⑰ _____

⑪ _____

⑫ _____

⑬ _____

⑱ _____

⑭ _____

⑮ _____

WINDOW ON GRAMMAR
Present Continuous Statements

⭐**A** Read the sentences.

> I **am wearing** a blue jacket.
> They **are wearing** red shoes.
> My friend **is wearing** black pants.

⭐**B** Complete the sentences.

1. I _____ wearing _____ .

2. The person next to me _____ wearing

   _____ .

3. Three people in the room _____ wearing

   _____ .

69

LESSON 2

I'm looking for children's clothes.

THINGS TO DO

1 Learn New Words

Look at the picture. Listen to the words. Then listen and repeat.

PEOPLE AND PLACES
1. department store
2. fitting room
3. customer
4. customer service
5. cashier
6. exit
7. entrance

ACTIONS
8. coming into
9. going into
10. talking
11. sleeping
12. leaving
13. running
14. buying

2 Practice the Conversation

Listen to the conversation. Then listen and repeat.

A: Where's Marc ?
B: He's near the exit .
A: What's he doing?
B: He's leaving the store .

Practice the conversation with a partner. Ask about these people.

1. Sam
2. Sara
3. Tom
4. Ed

3 Practice the Conversation

Listen to the conversation. Then listen and repeat.

A: Can I help you?
B: Yes, I'm looking for children's clothes .
A: They're on the second floor.
B: Thank you.

Practice the conversation with a partner. Ask about the places in the store directory.

STORE DIRECTORY

Children's Clothes	2nd floor
Children's Shoes	3rd floor
Women's Clothes	1st floor
Women's Coats	4th floor
Women's Shoes	3rd floor
Men's Clothes	1st floor
Men's Coats	4th floor
Men's Shoes	2nd floor
Sleepwear	3rd floor

Ed and Don

SCARVES

⭐3 LESSON

What size is it?

THINGS TO DO

1 Learn New Words 🎧

Look at the pictures. Listen to the words. Then listen and repeat.

① price tag　　③ size　　⑤ medium　　⑦ extra large
② receipt　　④ small　　⑥ large

2 Practice the Conversation 🎧

Listen to the conversation. Then listen and repeat.

A: What size is the `T-shirt` ?
B: It's `a small` .
A: Really? Is it on sale?
B: Yes. It's only `five dollars` .
A: Wow! `Five dollars` ! That's a good price.

Practice the conversation with a partner. Ask about these items.

1 sweater	2 blouse	3 coat	4 jacket	5 dress

★ ★

 TRY THIS Buy 3 things from Lane's Department Store.
Write the store receipt.

THANK YOU FOR SHOPPING AT
LANE'S DEPARTMENT STORE

_____

_____ _____

_____ _____

_____ _____

TOTAL _____

★ ★

SIZE: SMALL ①
$5.00
PRICE: $10.00

④

SIZE: MEDIUM
$20.00
PRICE: $40.00

③

SIZE: SMALL
$25.00
PRICE: $50.00

72

SALE
Lane's Department Store

SIZE: EXTRA LARGE
$15.00
PRICE: $30.00

⑦

⑤

SIZE: MEDIUM
$10.00
PRICE: $20.00

⑥

SIZE: LARGE
$30.00
PRICE: $60.00

THANK YOU FOR SHOPPING AT
LANE'S DEPARTMENT STORE

②

T-shirt	$5.00
Blouse	$10.00
Coat	$30.00
Sweater	$15.00
Jacket	$25.00
Dress	$20.00
SUB-TOTAL	**$105.00**
TAX	**$5.25**
TOTAL	**$110.25**

WINDOW ON MATH 🎧
Multiplying and Dividing

A Listen to the sentences. Then listen and repeat.

1. Six times two equals twelve. ($6 \times 2 = 12$)
2. Twelve times two equals twenty-four. ($12 \times 2 = 24$)
3. Six divided by two equals three. ($6 \div 2 = 3$)
4. Twelve divided by two equals six. ($12 \div 2 = 6$)

B Write the missing words.

1. Ten _____ two equals twenty.
2. Six _____ one equals six.
3. Four _____ by two equals two.
4. Four _____ four equals sixteen.
5. _____ times _____ equals _____.
6. _____ divided by _____ equals _____.

4 LESSON

A Folktale

This is a story about Simon and Leo. Simon is a tailor. Leo is his friend. One day Leo comes into Simon's store. Leo is wearing a very old coat.

LEO: Oh, Simon, there is a big hole in my coat. What can I do?

THINGS TO DO

1 Learn New Words 🎧

Look at the pictures. Listen to the words. Then listen and repeat.

① big hole   ③ scissors
② cutting   ④ tailor

2 Read 🎧

Look at the pictures. Listen to the story. Then complete the story chart.

STORY CHART

At the beginning of the story, Leo is wearing _____ .

⬇

Next, Leo is wearing _____ .

⬇

Five years later Leo is wearing _____ .

3 Predict 🎧

What is the missing word at the end of the story? Share ideas with your classmates. Then listen and compare.

At the end of the story, Leo is wearing ___**?**___ .

It is five years later.

LEO: Oh, Simon, there is a big hole in my jacket. What can I do?

Simon looks at the jacket carefully. Then he leaves the room. After an hour, he comes back.

SIMON: Here you are, Leo. Your old jacket is now a vest.

LEO: Oh, Simon, it's a beautiful vest. How can I thank you?

2

Simon looks at the coat carefully. Then he takes out his scissors.

LEO: What are you doing, Simon?

SIMON: I'm cutting up your coat.

3

Simon leaves the room with the pieces of Leo's coat. After an hour, he comes back.

SIMON: Here you are, Leo. Your old coat is now a jacket.

LEO: Oh, Simon, it's a beautiful jacket. How can I thank you?

5

It is five years later.

LEO: Oh, Simon, there is a big hole in my vest. What can I do?

Simon looks at the vest carefully. Then he leaves the room. After an hour, he comes back.

SIMON: Here you are, Leo. Your old vest is now a ___**?**___.

LEO: Oh, Simon, it's beautiful. How can I thank you?

WINDOW ON GRAMMAR
Object Pronouns:
me, you, him, her, it, them, us

> He is looking at <u>**me**</u>.
> I am looking at <u>**you**</u>.
> She is looking at <u>**him**</u>.
> He is looking at <u>**her**</u>.
> I am looking at <u>**it**</u>.
> She is looking at <u>**them**</u>.
> Our teacher is looking at <u>**us**</u>.

★ Complete the sentences *with me, you, him, her, it, them,* or *us*.

1. Leo is talking to Simon. He is asking

   _____ a question.

2. Simon is looking at Leo's coat. He is

   looking at _____ carefully.

3. She isn't closing the windows. She is

   opening _____.

5 LESSON

It's too short.

1 Learn New Words 🎧

Look at the pictures. Listen to the words. Then listen and repeat.

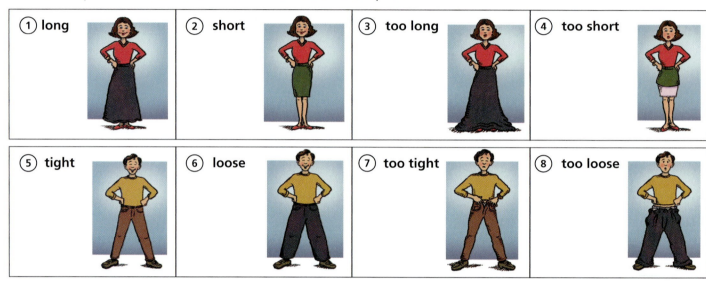

① long ② short ③ too long ④ too short

⑤ tight ⑥ loose ⑦ too tight ⑧ too loose

Describe the clothes in the pictures.

1. The black skirt isn't short. It's _____ .

2. The green skirt isn't too long. It's _____ .

3. The brown pants aren't loose. They're _____ .

4. The black pants aren't too tight. They're _____ .

2 Practice the Conversation: Describing Clothes 🎧

Listen to the conversation. Then listen and repeat.

A: Do you like this dress ?

B: It's nice, but I think it's too short .

Practice the conversation with a partner. Use these items.

 1 sweater — long

 2 jacket — tight

 3 hat — big

 4 blouse — loose

 5 💡

3 Practice the Conversation: Returning Something 🎧

Listen to the conversation. Then listen and repeat.

A: I'd like to return these pants .

B: What's the problem?

A: They're too short .

B: All right. No problem.

Practice the conversation with a partner.
Use these items.

1 shoes	2 pajamas	3 shorts	4 boots	5
tight	loose	tight	small	

WINDOW ON PRONUNCIATION 🎧
Vowel Sounds in *Shoes* and *Should*

A Listen to the words. Then listen and repeat.

1. shoes   (should)   loose   too

2. look   book   put   two

3. you   noon   woman   loose

4. boots   excuse   good   blue

Listen again. Circle the word that has a different vowel sound.

B Listen to the words. Then listen and repeat.

1. blue   a. book
2. good   b. June
3. cook   c. shoe
4. noon   d. should

Work with a partner. Match the words that have the same sound.

Work Clothes

1 Ask Questions

Work with a partner. Ask and answer questions about clothing. Use the names below.

A: What's Ken wearing?

B: He's wearing a green shirt, green pants, white shoes, and a white hat.

| Ken | Taka | Joe | Mei |

| 1 Taka | 2 Joe | 3 Mei | 4 our teacher | 5 |

2 Give Opinions

Work with a partner. Match Ken, Taka, Joe, and Mei to his or her occupation.

Occupations			
dentist	bus driver	teacher	nurse
librarian	police officer	pharmacist	cashier

A: What's Ken's occupation?

B: I think he is a _____.

A: Why?

B: Because he's wearing _____.

3 Read

Read the memo. Then complete the sentences about Leila, Phil, and Rob.

Smith Industries

Memo

To: All Employees
Topic: Work Clothes

From: Louis Smith
Date: August 1, 2004

All employees should dress appropriately. If your clothes are not appropriate, your supervisor may ask you to go home.

Inappropriate Work Clothes					
jeans		shorts or short skirts		baseball caps	
T-shirts		sneakers		sandals	

Leila

Leila's clothes are inappropriate for work because she is wearing

_____
_____
_____ .

Phil

Phil's clothes are inappropriate for work because he is wearing

_____
_____
_____ .

Rob

Rob's clothes are inappropriate for work because he is wearing

_____
_____
_____ .

7 LESSON

What do you know?

1 Listening Review 🎧

Listen and choose the correct answer. Use the Answer Sheet.

1. A. medium
   B. $15.00
   C. blue

2. A. a sweater
   B. brown
   C. at the department store

3. A. on the 2nd floor
   B. He's leaving.
   C. pajamas

4. A. red
   B. on sale
   C. a small

5. A. It's nice.
   B. Yes, it is.
   C. Thanks.

6. A. It's extra large.
   B. It's blue.
   C. fifty dollars

7. A. It's a green sweater.
   B. They're next to the elevator.
   C. They're too small.

8. A. Yes, it is.
   B. Yes, they are.
   C. Yes, there are.

ANSWER SHEET

1	A	B	C
2	A	B	C
3	A	B	C
4	A	B	C
5	A	B	C
6	A	B	C
7	A	B	C
8	A	B	C

2 Dictation 🎧

Listen and write the questions you hear.

1. _____

_____

2. _____

_____

3. _____

_____

Work with a partner. Ask and answer the questions.

3 Conversation Check: Pair Work

Student A: Go to page 166.

Student B: Ask your partner questions to complete the price tags.

EXAMPLE: **B:** What size is the blue sweater?

A: It's an extra large.

B: How much is it?

a. Size: LARGE Price: $40.00

b. Size: Extra Large Price:

c. Size: SMALL Price: $25.00

d. Size: Price:

✓	How many questions did you ask your partner?	How many questions did you answer?
	□ 1 □ 2 □ 3 □ 4	□ 1 □ 2 □ 3 □ 4

✓ LEARNING LOG

I know these words:

□ big
□ black
□ blouse
□ blue
□ boot
□ briefs
□ brown
□ buying
□ cap
□ coat
□ coming into
□ customer
□ customer service

□ cutting
□ department store
□ divided by
□ dress
□ entrance
□ exit
□ extra large
□ fitting room
□ going into
□ green
□ hat
□ hole

□ jacket
□ large
□ leaving
□ long
□ looking for
□ loose
□ medium
□ men
□ necktie
□ pajamas
□ pants
□ price
□ price tag

□ purple
□ receipt
□ red
□ running
□ scissors
□ shirt
□ shoe
□ short
□ shorts
□ size
□ skirt
□ sleeping
□ small

□ sock
□ sweater
□ tailor
□ talking to
□ tight
□ times
□ too
□ T-shirt
□ undershirt
□ wearing
□ white
□ women
□ yellow

I can ask:

□ What color is the jacket?
□ What's he doing?
□ What size is the shirt?
□ Do you like this dress?
□ What's the problem?
□ What's her occupation?

I can say:

□ I'm looking for children's clothes.
□ He's wearing a coat.
□ It's too short.
□ I'd like to return these pants.
□ $6 \times 2 = 12$
□ $12 \div 2 = 6$

I can write:

□ a store receipt

Spotlight: Grammar

PRESENT CONTINUOUS		
I	am am not	
You We They	are are not	working.
He She It	is is not	

1 Write *am*, *is*, or *are*.

1. Louis ____*is*____ reading in the library.

2. Tom and Tina _____ talking on the telephone.

3. Erik _____ wearing his new jacket.

4. I _____ reading a book.

5. You and I _____ sitting in class.

6. I _____ doing my homework.

7. We _____ eating lunch.

8. She _____ sitting at her desk.

2 Write about the people in the pictures.

1. _They are running._

2. _____

3. _____

4. _____

5. _____

6. _____

INFORMATION QUESTIONS WITH THE PRESENT CONTINUOUS

What	**is**	she reading?	What	**are**	you reading?
Where	**is**	he sitting?	Where	**are**	they sitting?
Why	**is**	Mr. Smith leaving?	Why	**are**	Mr. and Mrs. Smith leaving?
Who	**is**	sitting down?	Who	**are**	you talking to?

3 Match the questions and answers.

1. _d_ What is he doing?

2. ____ Where is she reading?

3. ____ Who are you talking to?

4. ____ Why are you wearing shorts?

5. ____ What are you watching?

a. my teacher

b. a movie

c. in her room

d. He's sleeping.

e. because it's hot

4 Complete the conversations. Then practice with a partner.

A: _____What_____ _____are_____ you reading?

B: I'm reading a library book.

A: _____ _____ she wearing?

B: She's wearing a blue dress.

A: _____ _____ they going?

B: They're going to Lane's Department Store.

A: _____ _____ you listening to?

B: We're listening to the radio.

A: _____ is sitting next to you?

B: _____

A: _____ are you sitting next to?

B: _____

Noodles are delicious.

THINGS TO DO

1 Learn New Words 🎧

Look at the pictures. Listen to the words. Then listen and repeat.

① noodles ⑧ bananas ⑮ shrimp
② bread ⑨ milk ⑯ beans
③ rice ⑩ cheese ⑰ onions
④ cereal ⑪ yogurt ⑱ tomatoes
⑤ apples ⑫ butter ⑲ lettuce
⑥ oranges ⑬ peanuts ⑳ carrots
⑦ grapes ⑭ chicken

Write the words next to the pictures. Then add another food to each group.

2 Give Opinions

Group the foods above. Put the words that end in -s in Group 1. Put the other words into Group 2.

GROUP 1	GROUP 2
noodles	bread

Work with a partner. Give your opinion of 5 foods.

I think noodles <u>are</u> delicious.

I think bread <u>is</u> good.

delicious   good   terrible

3 Write

Make a shopping list like this. Write 10 foods.

SHOPPING LIST	
Fruit & Vegetables apples	Dairy milk
Grains bread	Other

Grains

① noodles
② _____
③ _____
④ _____

_____

├── **FOOD**

Meat, Fish, Beans, Nuts

⑬ _____

⑭ _____

⑮ _____

⑯ _____

_____

Fruit

⑤ _____

⑥ _____

⑦ _____

⑧ _____

💡 _____

Dairy

⑨ _____

⑩ _____

⑪ _____

⑫ _____

💡 _____

GROUPS

Vegetables

⑰ _____

⑱ _____

⑲ _____

⑳ _____

💡 _____

WINDOW ON GRAMMAR
Questions with *Do you like*

⭐ **A** Read the questions and answers.

QUESTIONS	ANSWERS
Do you like rice?	Yes, I **do**.
Do you like cheese?	No, I **don't**.

⭐ **B** Work with a partner. Ask about 5 foods.

EXAMPLE:

A: Do you like <u>milk</u>?

B: <u>No, I don't.</u>

⭐ **C** Write a sentence about your partner. Read it to the class.

My partner likes _____ and _____ .

2 LESSON

Do you sell rice?

THINGS TO DO

1 Talk About the Picture

Write 5 things about the picture.

> EXAMPLES: Gail is looking at paper towels.
> Tina is standing in line.

Share your ideas with the class.

2 Learn New Words 🎧

Look at the picture. Listen to the words. Then listen and repeat.

1. Aisle 1
2. restroom
3. ice
4. frozen foods
5. produce section
6. shopping cart
7. mop
8. checkout counter
9. coupons
10. bakery
11. pushing a cart
12. looking at
13. eating
14. cleaning the floor
15. standing in line

3 Practice the Conversation 🎧

Listen to the conversations. Then listen and repeat.

A: Excuse me. Do you sell rice ?
B: Yes, we do. It's in Aisle 1 .
A: Thank you.
B: You're welcome.

A: Excuse me. Do you sell bananas ?
B: Yes, we do. They're in the produce section .
A: Thank you.
B: You're welcome.

Practice the conversations with a partner. Ask about these things.

UNIT 6: Food

How much is it?

THINGS TO DO

1 Learn New Words 🎧

Look at the picture. Listen to the words. Then listen and repeat.

① a bag of apples ⑤ a jar of honey ⑧ a bottle of oil
② a carton of milk ⑥ a box of sugar ⑨ expensive
③ a loaf of bread ⑦ a can of tomatoes ⑩ cheap
④ a package of cheese

What other foods are in the picture? Share ideas with your classmates.

2 Find Someone Who

Make a chart like this. Write 8 foods from the picture.

FOOD	PERSON'S NAME
1. a loaf of bread	Keiko
2. a jar of honey	Tina

Talk to your classmates. Find someone who has the food at home. Write the person's name.

A: Do you have a loaf of bread at home?

B: Yes, I do. / No, I don't.

3 Practice the Conversation 🎧

Listen to the conversation. Then listen and repeat.

A: Excuse me. How much is a loaf of bread ?

B: Five dollars.

A: Wow! That's expensive.

Practice the conversation with a partner. Ask about these foods.

88

WINDOW ON MATH
Pounds, Ounces, and Cups

1 pound (lb.) = 16 ounces (oz.)
1 cup (c.) = 8 fluid ounces (oz.)
16 tablespoons (tbsp) = 1 cup (c.)

A Answer the questions.

1. How many ounces are in two pounds of shrimp?

2. How many ounces are in a pound and a half of beans?

3. You have a half cup of milk. How many ounces is that?

4. You have a half pound of lettuce. How many ounces is that?

5. You need a half cup of oil. How many tablespoons is that?

Store Flyers

THINGS TO DO

1 Read

Read the store flyers. Write the price and amount of each food.

Food	Ray's Supermarket		Ford's Supermarket	
	Price	Amount	Price	Amount
green beans	$1.25	1 lb.		
chicken				
orange juice	$2.00	32 oz.		
vegetable oil				
carrots				

2 Compare

Where is the food cheaper? Check (✔) your answer.

	RAY'S	FORD'S
Green beans are cheaper at	☐	✔
Chicken is cheaper at	☐	☐
Orange juice is cheaper at	☐	☐
Vegetable oil is cheaper at	☐	☐
Carrots are cheaper at	☐	☐

★★★★★★★★★★★★★★★★★★★★★★★★★★★★★★

 TRY THIS You have $5.00 to buy food you see in the two store flyers. What do you want to buy? Where do you want to buy it?

Food	Store	Price
	Subtotal	

Ray's SUPERMARKET

1 20 per pound
• Chicken Legs

2 FOR $4
• Orange Juice
32 oz. carton

3 99
• Vegetable Oil
96 oz. bottle

2 FOR $6
• Carrots
5 lb. bag

1 25 per pound
• Fresh Green Beans

THE SUPER SAVER!

FORD'S SUPERMARKET

2⁹⁹ 16 oz. bottle
Vegetable Oil

1⁹⁹ 64 oz. carton
Orange Juice

99¢ a pound
Chicken Legs

99¢ per pound
Fresh Green Beans

79¢ per pound
Carrots

Prices That Can't Be Beat!

WINDOW ON GRAMMAR
Frequency Adverbs

A Read the numbers and words.

| 100% always | 70–90% usually | 20–40% sometimes | 0% never |

B Complete the sentences with *always, usually, sometimes,* or *never.*

1. I _____ eat rice in the morning.

2. I _____ eat lunch at noon.

3. I _____ eat dinner at 6:00 P.M.

4. I _____ eat cereal for dinner.

5. I _____ eat in a restaurant on Sunday.

Is milk on sale?

1 Practice the Conversation: Ordering Food at a Counter 🎧

Listen to the conversation. Then listen and repeat.

A: Number 27 , please.

B: That's me.

A: What can I get for you?

B: Three pounds of chicken.

A: Anything else?

B: No, that's all.

Practice the conversation with a partner.
Use these items.

1	28
	A pound

2	29
	Half a pound

3	30
	Two pounds

4

2 Practice the Conversation: Asking for Help 🎧

Listen to the conversation. Then listen and repeat.

A: Can I help you?

B: Yes. Do you have vegetable oil ?

A: Yes, we do. It's on sale this week.

B: How much is it?

A: $1.99 for a 64-ounce bottle.

Practice the conversation with a partner. Use these items.

1	cheese
	$2.25 for a
	10-ounce package.

2	white rice
	99¢ for a
	16-oz. bag.

3	bread
	$2.50 for a
	24-oz. loaf.

4

3 Practice the Conversation: Asking about Sales 🎧

Listen to the conversation. Then listen and repeat.

A: Is milk on sale this week?

B: Yes. It's only 99 cents a carton .

A: What size?

B: 32 ounces.

A: Wow! That's a good price.

Practice the conversation with a partner.
Use these items.

1 rice	**2** honey	**3** sugar	**4**
a bag / 12 ounces	a jar / 8 ounces	a box / 16 ounces	

WINDOW ON PRONUNCIATION 🎧
Intonation in *Yes/No* Questions

A Listen to the questions. Then listen and repeat.

1. Can I help you?

2. Do you have grape juice?

3. Is rice on sale this week?

4. Anything else?

5. Do you sell noodles?

6. Do you have a package of cheese at home?

7. Do you like apples?

Work with a partner. Ask and answer the questions.

B Listen to the sentences. Then listen and repeat.

1. A. The apples are on sale   2. A. Okay   3. A. Milk

   B. The apples are on sale   B. Okay   B. Milk

Listen again. Write a period after each statement and a question mark after each question.

UNIT 6: Food

The Food Pyramid

1 Talk About the Picture

What foods do you know in the picture below? What foods can you add to each group?

The Food Pyramid

Do you eat the right foods? This is one guide to help you choose foods that are good for you.

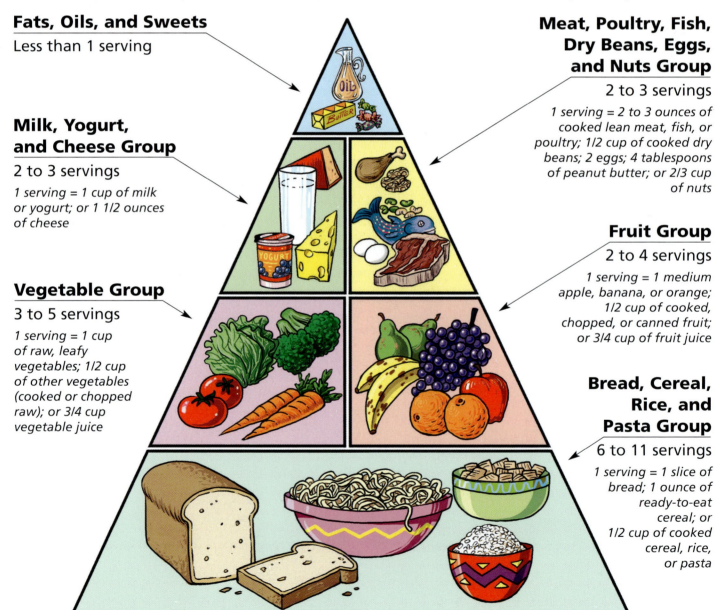

Fats, Oils, and Sweets
Less than 1 serving

Milk, Yogurt, and Cheese Group
2 to 3 servings

1 serving = 1 cup of milk or yogurt; or 1 1/2 ounces of cheese

Vegetable Group
3 to 5 servings

1 serving = 1 cup of raw, leafy vegetables; 1/2 cup of other vegetables (cooked or chopped raw); or 3/4 cup vegetable juice

Meat, Poultry, Fish, Dry Beans, Eggs, and Nuts Group
2 to 3 servings

1 serving = 2 to 3 ounces of cooked lean meat, fish, or poultry; 1/2 cup of cooked dry beans; 2 eggs; 4 tablespoons of peanut butter; or 2/3 cup of nuts

Fruit Group
2 to 4 servings

1 serving = 1 medium apple, banana, or orange; 1/2 cup of cooked, chopped, or canned fruit; or 3/4 cup of fruit juice

Bread, Cereal, Rice, and Pasta Group
6 to 11 servings

1 serving = 1 slice of bread; 1 ounce of ready-to-eat cereal; or 1/2 cup of cooked cereal, rice, or pasta

2 Read

Study the food pyramid. Complete this chart.

FOOD GROUP	NUMBER OF SERVINGS PER DAY
1. *Bread, Cereal, Rice, and Pasta Group*	*6 to 11*
2. *Fruit Group*	
3.	
4.	
5.	
6.	

3 Write

Write the number of servings.

1 2 slices of bread = _____2 servings_____	2 4 eggs = _____	3 1½ cups of orange juice = _____
4 1 cup of cooked dry beans = _____	5 1 cup of uncooked or raw spinach = _____	6 1 cup of cooked rice = _____

★★

 TRY THIS Write 4 sentences about you and people in your family.

EXAMPLES: *I eat about 5 servings of vegetables every day.*
My father always eats 1 serving of pasta at night.
I usually eat 1 serving of yogurt in the morning.
My son eats 2 servings of fruit in the evening.

★★

7 LESSON

What do you know?

1 Listening Review 🎧

Listen and choose the word you hear. Use the Answer Sheet.

1. A. always   B. sometimes   C. never
2. A. usually   B. sometimes   C. never
3. A. always   B. usually   C. never
4. A. always   B. sometimes   C. never

Listen and choose the best answer. Use the Answer Sheet.

5. A. Yes, I do.
   B. $5 a pound
   C. in Aisle 3

6. A. at the checkout counter
   B. Yes, we do.
   C. That's right.

7. A. It's delicious.
   B. It's $3.99.
   C. in Aisle 1

8. A. 16 ounces
   B. $1.99
   C. Yes, it is.

9. A. No, it isn't.
   B. a 12-ounce bag
   C. orange juice

10. A. That's a good price.
    B. a pound of chicken
    C. It's delicious.

ANSWER SHEET

1 Ⓐ Ⓑ Ⓒ
2 Ⓐ Ⓑ Ⓒ
3 Ⓐ Ⓑ Ⓒ
4 Ⓐ Ⓑ Ⓒ
5 Ⓐ Ⓑ Ⓒ
6 Ⓐ Ⓑ Ⓒ
7 Ⓐ Ⓑ Ⓒ
8 Ⓐ Ⓑ Ⓒ
9 Ⓐ Ⓑ Ⓒ
10 Ⓐ Ⓑ Ⓒ

2 Dictation 🎧

Listen and write the missing words.

Attention, shoppers.

If you like _____ for breakfast, *Corn Crunch* is on sale today. It's

only $3.95 for a _____ box. With _____

and _____, your breakfast will be _____

and nutritious. The bananas are in the _____ section,

and the milk is in the _____ section.

3 Conversation Check: Pair Work

Student A: Go to page 166.

Student B: Ask your partner questions to complete this chart.

EXAMPLE: **B:** How much is a can of tomatoes?

A: $2.50

	FOOD	PRICE (How much?)	SIZE/AMOUNT (What size?)
1		$2.50	
2			
3		$2.00	48 ounces
4		$6.00	32 ounces

✔	How many questions did you ask your partner?	How many questions did you answer?
	□ 1 □ 2 □ 3 □ 4	□ 1 □ 2 □ 3 □ 4

✔ LEARNING LOG

I know these words:

□ aisle	□ cheap	□ frozen foods	□ mop	□ restroom
□ always	□ checkout counter	□ fruit	□ never	□ rice
□ apple	□ cheese	□ grain	□ noodles	□ serving
□ bag	□ chicken	□ grape	□ nut	□ shopping cart
□ bakery	□ clean the floor	□ have	□ oil	□ shrimp
□ banana	□ cooked	□ honey	□ onion	□ slice
□ bean	□ coupon	□ ice	□ on sale	□ sometimes
□ bottle	□ cup	□ jar	□ orange	□ stand in line
□ box	□ dairy	□ juice	□ ounce	□ sugar
□ bread	□ delicious	□ lettuce	□ package	□ terrible
□ butter	□ eat	□ like	□ peanut	□ tomato
□ can	□ egg	□ loaf	□ pound	□ usually
□ carrot	□ expensive	□ look at	□ produce section	□ vegetable
□ carton	□ fish	□ meat	□ push a cart	□ yogurt
□ cereal	□ food	□ milk	□ raw	

I can ask:

□ Do you like noodles?
□ Do you sell rice?
□ How much is a loaf of bread?
□ What can I get for you?
□ Is milk on sale?

I can say:

□ Yes, I do.
□ No, I don't.
□ It's 99¢.
□ A pound of chicken, please.
□ It's in Aisle 3.

I can write:

□ food words
□ sentences about a supermarket
□ the price of foods
□ a shopping list
□ sentences about eating habits

Spotlight: Writing

1 Read the recipe. Number the pictures in order from first (1) to last (5).

RECIPE

My Favorite Soup
Lucy Kimball

Ingredients

1 lb. broccoli
1 lb. potatoes
water
salt
pepper

Directions

Wash the broccoli and the potatoes. Cut the potatoes in quarters and put them in a large pot with water. Boil the potatoes for about 20 minutes. Add the broccoli and boil for 3 minutes. Put the broccoli and the potatoes into a blender. Add some of the water and blend. Add salt and pepper and serve hot.

Boil the broccoli for 3 minutes.

Wash the vegetables.

Blend the vegetables with some water.

Add salt and pepper and serve hot.

Cut up the potatoes and boil them for 20 minutes.

2 Connect the sentences. Use *and*.

1. Cook it for 30 minutes. Serve it hot.

Cook it for 30 minutes and serve it hot.

2. Put the vegetables in a blender. Blend them.

_____

_____

3. Add the broccoli. Boil it for 3 minutes.

_____

4. Cut the potatoes in quarters. Boil them.

_____

5. Put water in a large pot. Add salt.

_____

6. Cook the vegetables. Serve them hot.

_____

FOCUS ON WRITING: Connecting Sentences

Use *and* to connect two sentences.

Examples:

Cut up the potatoes. Put them in a large pot.
Cut up the potatoes **and** put them in a large pot.

Add the broccoli. Cook it for 3 minutes.
Add the broccoli **and** cook it for 3 minutes.

---

3 Choose a favorite recipe. Write the ingredients. Write the directions.

_____

_____

Ingredients

Directions

LESSON 1

What's your brother's name?

THINGS TO DO

1 Learn New Words 🎧

Look at the pictures of this family. Listen to the words. Then listen and repeat.

1. husband
2. wife
3. parents
4. children
5. mother
6. daughter
7. father
8. son
9. sister
10. brother
11. grandmother
12. grandson
13. grandfather
14. granddaughter

Make a chart like this. Write the family words.

MALES	FEMALES	MALES OR FEMALES
husband	wife	parents

2 Write

Add names to Ann's family tree.

Carol
Grandmother   Grandfather

Father   Mother

Ann

Brother

★ ★

 TRY THIS Interview a classmate and take notes. Then make a family tree for your partner. For example, ask:

What's your mother's name?
What is your grandmother's name?

★ ★

1 Jack   2 Mei

3 Jack and Mei   4 Ann and Tim

5 Mei   6 Ann

WINDOW ON GRAMMAR
Yes/No Questions + Simple Present

A Read the questions and answers.

QUESTIONS	ANSWERS
Do you live with your wife?	Yes, I **do**.
Do you have children?	No, we **don't**.
Do your parents live with you?	No, they **don't**.
Does your wife have a sister?	Yes, she **does**.
Does your brother live here?	No, he **doesn't**.

B Complete the questions with *Do* or *Does*. Then ask a partner.

1. _____ you live with your grandparents?

2. _____ your father live near you?

3. _____ your parents live in the United States?

4. _____ you have children?

5. _____ your grandmother live in this country?

2 LESSON

I usually cook dinner.

THINGS TO DO

1 Learn New Words 🎧

Look at the pictures. Listen to the words. Then listen and repeat.

① **fix things**		⑥ **pay the bills**
② **make the bed**		⑦ **clean the house**
③ **wash the dishes**		⑧ **do the laundry**
④ **take out the trash**		⑨ **cook dinner**
⑤ **buy the groceries**			

Write the words under the pictures.

2 Interview

Work with a partner. Ask the questions below. Check (✓) your partner's answers.

DO YOU _____?	YES, OFTEN.	YES, SOMETIMES.	NO, NEVER.
fix things at home	☐	☐	☐
make the beds	☐	☐	☐
wash the dishes	☐	☐	☐
take out the trash	☐	☐	☐
buy the groceries	☐	☐	☐
pay the bills	☐	☐	☐
clean the house	☐	☐	☐
do the laundry	☐	☐	☐

Share 3 things about your partner with the class.

> EXAMPLE: My partner often does the laundry.

3 Write

What do *you* do at home? Write your answer.

> EXAMPLE:
> I usually cook dinner and clean the house. I sometimes wash the dishes and take out the trash. I never pay the bills.

① _____ *fix things*

⑨ _____

⑧ _____

3 _____

4 _____

Family Responsibilities

5 _____

6 _____

WINDOW ON GRAMMAR
Simple Present Statements

A Read the sentences.

I **cook** dinner.	He **cooks** dinner.
You **wash** the dishes.	Jon **washes** the dishes.
We **make** the beds.	She **makes** the bed.
They **fix** things.	Ann **fixes** things.

B Complete these sentences.

1. Her brother _____ the dishes on Sunday.

2. He often _____ dinner on Saturday.

3. Mei's husband always _____ the groceries.

4. Their children _____ _____ the trash.

5. Tim's parents _____ the laundry.

C Write 4 sentences about people in your family.

EXAMPLE: My husband never fixes things at home.

103

LESSON 3

What do you do for fun?

THINGS TO DO

1 Talk About the Picture

Write 5 things about the picture.

> EXAMPLE: The big white dog is running.

Share your ideas with the class.

2 Learn New Words 🎧

Look at the picture. Listen to the words. Then listen and repeat.

1. read the newspaper
2. play an instrument
3. dance
4. play cards
5. take pictures
6. listen to music
7. play soccer
8. tell stories

3 Interview

Ask your partner the questions below. Check (✓) your partner's answers.

DOES YOUR FAMILY _____?	YES, OFTEN.	YES, SOMETIMES.	NO, NEVER.
listen to music	☐	☐	☐
play cards	☐	☐	☐
play instruments	☐	☐	☐
tell stories	☐	☐	☐
play soccer	☐	☐	☐

Share 3 things about your partner with the class.

> EXAMPLE: My partner's family often plays cards.

★★★★★★★★★★★★★★★★★★★★★★★★★★★★★★★★★★★★★

TRY THIS Write 3 questions. Then ask a partner your questions.

Who in your family _____*plays cards*_____ ?

Who in your family _____ ?

Who in your family _____ ?

★★★★★★★★★★★★★★★★★★★★★★★★★★★★★★★★★★★★★

Family Portraits

THINGS TO DO

1 Read and Take Notes

Read about each family. Take notes in the chart below.

NAME	MARITAL STATUS	LIVES WITH
1. Pilar	married	husband and 2 children
2. Boris		
3. Sonya		
4. Nhu Trinh		

Work with a partner. Tell about each person's family.

EXAMPLE: Pilar is married and she lives with her husband and two children.

2 Write

Write about people in your family.

1. My aunt's name is _____ .

   She is my _____ sister.

2. My uncle's name is _____ .

   He is my _____ brother.

3. I live with _____ .

★★★★★★★★★★★★★★★★★★★★★★★★★★★★★★★★★

TRY THIS Write 3 or more sentences about your family.

My name is _____ .

I'm from _____ . I live with

_____ .

★★★★★★★★★★★★★★★★★★★★★★★★★★★★★★★★★

1 My name is Pilar Garcia and I'm from Mexico. I am married and I have two children. My husband's name is Manuel. My two daughters' names are Belen and Maria. They are 12 and 14. We live together in Phoenix, and we are very happy.

4 My name is Nhu Trinh. I'm from Vietnam. I have three children. My husband and I live in California. I work at a bank in Los Angeles. My daughter and son-in-law live in Vietnam. My sons live in Arizona. I love my family, but we don't see each other very much.

2 My name is Boris and I'm from Russia. My wife's name is Anna. We have three children and two grandchildren. Now we live in a beautiful home with our daughter. My family is my whole life. I love my family.

3 My name is Sonya and I'm from China. I'm single. I live with my aunt and uncle. My uncle is my mother's brother. My mother and father live in China. I miss them very much.

WINDOW ON GRAMMAR
Don't and *Doesn't*

A Read the sentences.

I **don't** have children.	He **doesn't** have a sister.
We **don't** have children.	She **doesn't** have a son.
You **don't** have children.	
They **don't** have a daughter.	

B Complete these sentences with *don't* or *doesn't*.

1. I _____ have 20 children.
2. Her sister _____ have any children.
3. His parents _____ live in Canada.
4. Her children _____ live near her.
5. Their son _____ have a job.
6. My husband and I _____ live together.

5
LESSON

Just a minute, please.

1 Practice the Conversation: Making a Call

Listen to the conversation. Then listen and repeat.

A: Is Sam there?

B: I think you have the wrong number.

A: Is this 555-1212 ?

B: No, it isn't.

A: Sorry to bother you.

B: No problem. Bye.

Practice the conversation with a partner.
Use these items.

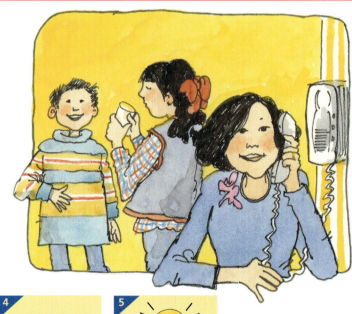

1	2	3	4	5
Anna / 555-4938	Mr. Wu / 555-3957	Lisa / 555-2468	Ms. Fallon / 555-3000	

2 Practice the Conversation: Answering the Phone

Listen to the conversation. Then listen and repeat.

A: Is Ann there?

B: Who's calling please?

A: This is Pat . I'm her classmate .

B: Just a minute, please. I'll get her.

Practice the conversation with a partner.
Use these items.

1	2	3	4	5
Sue / I play soccer with her.	Dan / I'm her teacher.	Maria / I play cards with her.	Dr. Smith / I'm her dentist.	

3 Practice the Conversation: Taking a Message

Listen to the conversation. Then listen and repeat

A: Can I speak to your father, please?

B: He's not here now. Can I take a message?

A: Can you ask him to call Mr. Rogers ?
My number is 555-3598 .

B: Call Mr. Rogers at 555-3598 .

A: Right. Thank you.

B: You're welcome. Good-bye.

Practice the conversation with a partner.
Use these items

1	Jeff / 555-2764	2	Dr. Smith / 555-4930	3	Ms. Tanaka / 555-0217	4	Mrs. Garcia / 555-1020	5	
	Jeff / 555-2764		Dr. Smith / 555-4930		Ms. Tanaka / 555-0217		Mrs. Garcia / 555-1020		

WINDOW ON PRONUNCIATION
Linking Consonant to Vowel

A Listen to the words. Then listen and repeat.

1. Sam is	4. I'm her	7. with Ann
2. ask him	5. can I	8. just a
3. this is	6. is Ann	

B Listen to the sentences. Then listen and repeat.

1. Can I speak to Mike Elliot, please?

2. Can you ask him to call Pat Adams?

3. My number is 555–1234.

4. Wait a minute.

5. His name is Bob Underwood.

Work with a partner. Circle the linking words in the sentences above.

EXAMPLE: 1. (Can I) speak to (Mike Elliot), please?

109

The Garcia Family's Expenses

1 Learn New Words 🎧

Look at the pictures below. Listen to the words. Then listen and repeat.

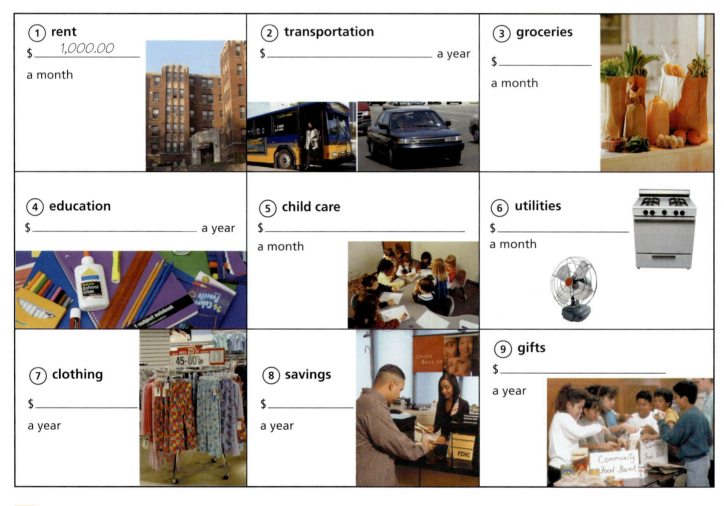

① **rent**
$ ___1,000.00___
a month

② **transportation**
$ _____ a year

③ **groceries**
$ _____
a month

④ **education**
$ _____ a year

⑤ **child care**
$ _____
a month

⑥ **utilities**
$ _____
a month

⑦ **clothing**
$ _____
a year

⑧ **savings**
$ _____
a year

⑨ **gifts**
$ _____
a year

2 Give Opinions 🎧

Work with a partner. How much does the Garcia family spend on their expenses? Use these amounts.
Write your ideas above.

$75.00	$240.00	$800.00	$1,000.00	$2,000.00
$200.00	$300.00	$900.00	$1,500.00	

Listen to a conversation with Mr. Garcia. Check your guesses.

3 Answer the Questions

Work with a partner. Answer the questions below.

1. How much does the Garcia family spend every year? Write the amounts below.

   rent for a year: _$1,000.00 × 12 = $12,000.00_____

   transportation for a year: _____

   groceries for a year: _____

   education for a year: _____

   child care for a year: _____

   utilities for a year: _____

   clothing for a year: _____

   Total: _____

2. Write the Garcia's yearly expenses in order from the most expensive to the least expensive.

   most expensive
   ($$$$)   _____rent_____

                 _____

                 _____

                 _____

                 _____

                 _____

   least expensive
   ($)   _____

3. What other expenses do you think the Garcias have? Share ideas with your class.

4 Make a Budget

What are your expenses? Complete the chart below.

MY EXPENSES	AMOUNT/MONTH	AMOUNT/YEAR
groceries	$400.00	$4,800.00
	Total:	

What do you know?

1 Listening Review 🎧

Look at the family tree. Listen and choose the best answer. Use the Answer Sheet.

1. A. Bob
   B. Jack
   C. Stephan

2. A. She's Jack's daughter.
   B. She's Jack's wife.
   C. She's Jack's mother.

3. A. She's Tim's mother.
   B. She's Tim's grandmother.
   C. She's Tim's sister.

4. A. Carol
   B. Mei
   C. Ann

Listen and choose the best answer. Use the Answer Sheet.

5. A. No, I don't.
   B. Yes, they do.
   C. Yes, she does.

6. A. It's John.
   B. He's my brother.
   C. He lives in New York.

7. A. Yes, they do.
   B. Yes, there are.
   C. Yes, he does.

8. A. She's my daughter.
   B. She makes the beds.
   C. My children do.

9. A. He lives with me.
   B. They live in New York.
   C. Yes, they are.

10. A. No, she doesn't.
    B. She cooks dinner.
    C. She lives in Florida.

11. A. Yes, I do.
    B. She doesn't.
    C. Yes, please.

12. A. They do.
    B. They often do.
    C. in the morning

	ANSWER SHEET		
1	Ⓐ	Ⓑ	Ⓒ
2	Ⓐ	Ⓑ	Ⓒ
3	Ⓐ	Ⓑ	Ⓒ
4	Ⓐ	Ⓑ	Ⓒ
5	Ⓐ	Ⓑ	Ⓒ
6	Ⓐ	Ⓑ	Ⓒ
7	Ⓐ	Ⓑ	Ⓒ
8	Ⓐ	Ⓑ	Ⓒ
9	Ⓐ	Ⓑ	Ⓒ
10	Ⓐ	Ⓑ	Ⓒ
11	Ⓐ	Ⓑ	Ⓒ
12	Ⓐ	Ⓑ	Ⓒ

2 Conversation Check: Pair Work

Student A: Go to page 167.

Student B: Ask your partner questions to complete this chart.

EXAMPLE: **B:** Who's John?

A: He's Bob's father.

		Bob's Family	
Name	**Relationship**	**Where does he/she live?**	**What does he/she do for fun?**
1. John	Bob's father	California	
2. Cora	Bob's grandmother		plays cards
3. Jodie		California	
4. Lisa	Bob's wife	Florida	plays the guitar
5. Beth	Bob's sister		plays basketball
6. Richard	Bob's brother	Florida	

✔

How many questions did you ask your partner?	How many questions did you answer?
☐ 1 ☐ 2 ☐ 3 ☐ 4 ☐ 5 ☐ 6 ☐ 7	☐ 1 ☐ 2 ☐ 3 ☐ 4 ☐ 5 ☐ 6 ☐ 7

✔ LEARNING LOG

I know these words:

- ☐ aunt
- ☐ brother
- ☐ budget
- ☐ buy the groceries
- ☐ child care
- ☐ children
- ☐ clean the house
- ☐ clothing
- ☐ cook dinner
- ☐ dance
- ☐ daughter

- ☐ do the laundry
- ☐ education
- ☐ expense
- ☐ father
- ☐ fix things
- ☐ gift
- ☐ granddaughter
- ☐ grandfather
- ☐ grandmother
- ☐ grandson
- ☐ groceries

- ☐ husband
- ☐ listen to music
- ☐ make the bed
- ☐ mother
- ☐ parents
- ☐ pay the bills
- ☐ play an instrument
- ☐ play cards
- ☐ play soccer
- ☐ read the newspaper
- ☐ rent

- ☐ savings
- ☐ sister
- ☐ son
- ☐ take out the trash
- ☐ take pictures
- ☐ tell stories
- ☐ transportation
- ☐ uncle
- ☐ utilities
- ☐ wash the dishes
- ☐ wife

I can ask:

- ☐ What's your mother's name?
- ☐ Do you live with your parents?
- ☐ Does he have children?
- ☐ Does your family play cards?
- ☐ Who's calling, please?

I can say:

- ☐ No, I don't.
- ☐ Yes, he does.
- ☐ I usually cook dinner.
- ☐ He washes the dishes.

I can write:

- ☐ about my family
- ☐ a budget

Spotlight: Grammar

SIMPLE PRESENT STATEMENTS

Regular verbs

I
You   **live** in California.   He   **lives** in Illinois.
We   **don't live** in New York.   She   **doesn't live** in Maine.
They

Irregular verbs

I
You   **have** two sisters.   He   **has** two sisters.
We   **don't have** two brothers.   She   **doesn't have** two brothers.
They

1 Complete the sentences. Write *don't* or *doesn't*.

1. My sister lives with my mother. She _____ *doesn't* _____ live with me.

2. We eat a lot of rice. We _____ eat a lot of bread.

3. I have three sons. I _____ have any daughters.

4. I go to work from Monday to Friday. I _____ go to work on Saturday.

5. My daughter goes to school in the morning. She _____ go to school in the afternoon.

6. I get up early in the morning. I _____ get up late.

7. John always has a big breakfast. He _____ have a big dinner.

2 Complete the conversations. Then practice with a partner.

1. A: Do you live with your parents?

   B: No, I _____ *don't* _____ . I
      _____ *live* _____ with my brother.

2. A: Do you have a job?

   B: Yes, I _____ .
      I _____ a job in a bank.

3. A: Does your father live here?

   B: No, he _____ .
      He _____ in China.

4. A: Do you usually cook dinner?

   B: No, I _____ . My
      husband usually _____ dinner.

INFORMATION QUESTIONS WITH THE SIMPLE PRESENT

What	**do**	I need for school?	What	**does**	he need for school?
Where	**do**	you live?	Where	**does**	she live?
When	**do**	they usually leave?	When	**does**	it usually leave?
Why	**do**	you live there?	Why	**does**	he live there?
Who	**do**	we know in Miami?	Who	**does**	she live with?
How many sisters	**do**	they have?	How many sisters	**does**	your mother have?

3 Complete the questions. Write *do* or *does*. Then answer the questions.

1. Where _____ *does* _____ your teacher live?

2. When _____ you leave class?

3. How many brothers _____ your mother have?

4. Who _____ you usually eat dinner with?

5. What _____ your family do for fun?

6. How much _____ a pound of chicken cost?

4 Write 4 questions. Then ask a classmate.

1. Where _____

_____

2. When _____

_____

3. Why _____

_____

4. Who _____

_____

LESSON 1

Head, Shoulders, Knees, and Toes

THINGS TO DO

1 Learn New Words 🎧

Look at the picture. Listen to the words. Then listen and repeat.

① head	⑧ toe	⑮ nose
② neck	⑨ ankle	⑯ ear
③ shoulder	⑩ knee	⑰ mouth
④ arm	⑪ stomach	⑱ chest
⑤ hand	⑫ throat	⑲ back
⑥ leg	⑬ eye	⑳ wrist
⑦ foot*	⑭ elbow	㉑ finger

*Note: The plural of *foot* is *feet*.

2 Write

Add the words above to this chart.

I have one . . .	I have two . . .	I have ten . . .
head	*arms*	

3 Practice the Conversation 🎧

Listen to the conversation. Then listen and repeat.

A: What's the problem?
B: My knee hurts.
A: Is it broken?
B: No, I don't think so.

Practice the conversation with a partner. Use these body parts.

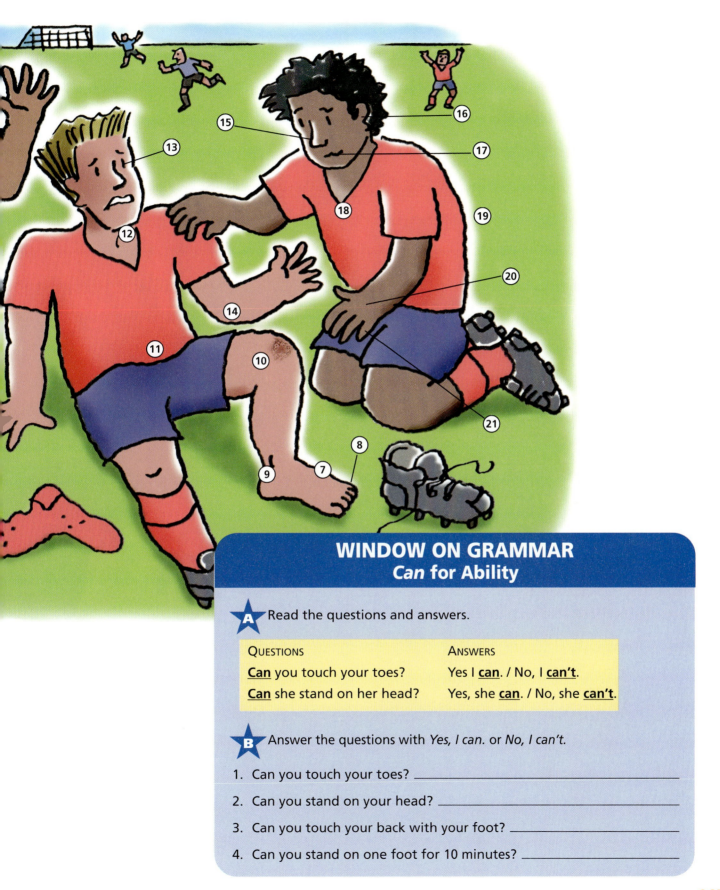

WINDOW ON GRAMMAR
Can for Ability

A Read the questions and answers.

QUESTIONS	ANSWERS
Can you touch your toes?	Yes I **can**. / No, I **can't**.
Can she stand on her head?	Yes, she **can**. / No, she **can't**.

B Answer the questions with *Yes, I can.* or *No, I can't.*

1. Can you touch your toes? _____

2. Can you stand on your head? _____

3. Can you touch your back with your foot? _____

4. Can you stand on one foot for 10 minutes? _____

2 LESSON

I have a bad headache.

THINGS TO DO

1 Talk About the Picture

Write 5 things about the picture. Share your ideas with the class.

> EXAMPLES: Tina is talking to the nurse.
> There's a clock in the room.

2 Learn New Words 🎧

Look at the picture. Listen to the words. Then listen and repeat.

① headache   ④ runny nose   ⑦ backache
② earache   ⑤ cough   ⑧ stomachache
③ fever   ⑥ sore throat

Work with a partner. Ask about the people in the picture.

A: What's the problem with Erik ?

B: He has a backache .

1	2	3	4
Tom	Tina	Ken	Donna

3 Practice the Conversation 🎧

Listen to the conversation. Then listen and repeat.

A: What's the problem?

B: I have a bad headache .

A: Does your throat hurt, too?

B: No, it doesn't.

Practice the conversation with a partner. Use these items.

3 LESSON

Put ice on it.

① _____ Drink liquids.

THINGS TO DO

1 Learn New Words 🎧

Look at the pictures. Listen to the words. Then listen and repeat.

① **Drink liquids.**
② **Eat soft food.**
③ **Take cough medicine.**
④ **Take aspirin.**
⑤ **Use ear drops.**

⑥ **Rest.**
⑦ **Put heat on it.**
⑧ **Put ice on it.**
⑨ **Bandage it.**
⑩ **Keep it dry.**

Write the words above the pictures.

⑩ _____

2 Interview

Interview a partner. Write your partner's answers.

What do you do for a _____ ?	
stomachache	_eat rice_
headache	_____
sore throat	_____
cough	_____
backache	_____

⑨ _____

Share your partner's answers with the class.

EXAMPLE: **My partner eats rice for a stomachache.**

3 Practice the Conversation 🎧

Listen to the conversation.
Then listen and repeat.

A: What's the problem?
B: I have a sore throat .
A: Are you drinking liquids ?
B: Yes, I am.

Practice the conversation
with a partner. Use these
problems.

⑧ _____

③ _____

④ _____

⑤ _____

⑥ _____

⑦ _____

WINDOW ON GRAMMAR
Giving Advice with *Should* and *Shouldn't*

A Read these sentences.

> You **should** go to the doctor.   You **shouldn't** put heat on it.
> You **should** put ice on it.   You **shouldn't** take aspirin.

B Complete the sentences with *should* or *shouldn't*.

1. You _____ use ear drops for a stomachache.
2. You _____ take cough medicine for a headache.
3. You _____ eat soft food for a stomachache.
4. You _____ put cough medicine on a sore knee.

C Write 2 more sentences.

You should _____.

You shouldn't _____.

121

UNIT 8: Health

4 LESSON

Safety Warnings

THINGS TO DO

1 Learn New Words 🎧

Look at the pictures below. Listen to the words. Then listen and repeat.

① Flammable!	② Poison!	③ Do not take internally.
④ Keep out of reach of children.	⑤ Pregnant women should not use this.	

Write the safety warnings under the pictures.

2 Read

Read the warning labels. Check (✓) True or False.

	True	False
1. Children should take aspirin for the flu.	☐	☑
2. Paint remover is flammable.	☐	☐
3. Bleach is a poison.	☐	☐
4. Pregnant women shouldn't use bleach.	☐	☐
5. You should keep ammonia out of reach of children.	☐	☐

3 Write

Make a chart like this. Work with a partner. Write 4 things on each side of the chart.

Things that are poisonous	Things you should keep out of reach of children
gasoline	

① _____

② _____

⑤ _____

_____

122

③ _____

④ _____

_____

WINDOW ON MATH
Gallons, Quarts, Pints, Cups, and Ounces

gallon   quart   pint   cup

1 gallon (gal.)	=	4 quarts (qt.)
1 quart (qt.)	=	2 pints (pt.)
1 pint (pt.)	=	2 cups (c.) = 16 fluid ounces (fl. oz.)

A Complete the sentences.

1. 2 quarts = 4 pints = _____8_____ cups = _____ ounces

2. 1 gallon = 4 quarts = _____ pints = _____ cups

3. 2 gallons = _____ quarts = _____ pints = _____ounces

B Answer the questions.

Which bottle should you buy?
Why?

LESSON 5

I need an ambulance.

1 Learn New Words

Look at the pictures below. Listen to the words. Then listen and repeat.

① **He is choking.**

② **He is bleeding.**

③ **She is having a heart attack.**

④ **She isn't breathing.**

2 Practice the Conversation: Calling 911

Listen to the conversation. Then listen and repeat.

A: This is 911.

B: We need an ambulance quickly. My friend is bleeding.

A: Where are you?

B: At the corner of Pine and Main.

Practice the conversation with a partner.
Use these items.

1	2	3	4
My friend is choking. / At 4533 Third Street.	A customer is having a heart attack. / At Lane's Department Store, on 12th Street.	My mother isn't breathing. / At 175 Main Street.	

3 Practice the Conversation: Deciding What to Do

Listen to the conversation. Then listen and repeat.

A: What's the problem?

B: Don has a bad cough . Should I call 911?

A: No. That's not an emergency.

Practice the conversation with a partner.
Use these items.

1 isn't breathing	2 has a fever of 100	3 has an earache	4 is having a heart attack	5
Yes, right away.	?	?	?	

WINDOW ON PRONUNCIATION
Linking Vowel to Vowel with a *Y* or *W* Sound

A Listen to the words. Then listen and repeat.

1. he is	5. we are	9. go on	13. you are
2. I am	6. try another	10. play it	14. she is
3. they are	7. who is	11. how are	15. do it
4. go up	8. who are	12. we own	16. day off

Write the words in the correct place.

Linking with a *y* sound		Linking with a *w* sound	
a. *he is* f.		a. *go on* e.	
b. g.		b. f.	
c. h.		c. g.	
d. i.		d.	
e. j.			

B Listen and complete the conversations.

1. A: This is 911.

   B: My mother is hurt. _____ choking.

   A: Where are you?

   B: _____ at 414 Pine Street.

2. A: Where are you?

   B: _____ at home.

   A: How's Paul?

   B: _____ resting.

6

LESSON

Places at a Hospital

1 Learn New Words 🎧

Look at the pictures. Listen to the words. Then listen and repeat.

(1) **Main Entrance**

(2) **Emergency Entrance**

(3) **Lobby**

(4) **Visitors' Lounge**

2 Talk About the Pictures

Write 5 things about the pictures above.

> EXAMPLES: People are sitting in the visitors' lounge.
> A boy is running near the main entrance.

Share your ideas with a partner.

3 Read the Map

Study the map. Check (✓) Yes or No.

	Yes	No
1. Is the main entrance on Perryridge Road?	✓	☐
2. Is the staff parking lot in front of the hospital?	☐	☐
3. Is the visitor parking lot next to the emergency entrance?	☐	☐
4. Is the Emergency Center at the front of the hospital?	☐	☐
5. Is Radiology to the right of the main entrance?	☐	☐
6. Is the lobby near the main entrance?	☐	☐
7. Is there a phone in the lounge?	☐	☐
8. Is there a restroom in the lobby?	☐	☐
9. Are there stairs in the lobby?	☐	☐
10. Are there two elevators?	☐	☐

7
LESSON

What do you know?

1 Listening Review 🎧

Listen to the conversations. Choose the problem you hear. Use the Answer Sheet.

ANSWER SHEET			
1	Ⓐ	Ⓑ	Ⓒ
2	Ⓐ	Ⓑ	Ⓒ
3	Ⓐ	Ⓑ	Ⓒ
4	Ⓐ	Ⓑ	Ⓒ
5	Ⓐ	Ⓑ	Ⓒ
6	Ⓐ	Ⓑ	Ⓒ
7	Ⓐ	Ⓑ	Ⓒ
8	Ⓐ	Ⓑ	Ⓒ

1.

A

B

C

2.

A

B

C

3.

A

B

C

4.

A

B

C

Listen and choose the best answer. Use the Answer Sheet.

5. A. Take cough medicine.
   B. Use eardrops.
   C. Put ice on it.

6. A. Bandage it.
   B. Eat soft food.
   C. Keep it dry.

7. A. 919
   B. 991
   C. 911

8. A. Yes, you should.
   B. Yes, you can.
   C. No, you shouldn't.

2 Conversation Check: Pair Work

Student A: Go to page 167.

Student B: Ask your partner questions to complete this chart.

EXAMPLE: **B:** What's the matter with Tom?

A: He has a sore neck.

B: What's he doing for it?

Name	What's the matter with him/her?	What's he/she doing for it?
1. Tom	He has a sore neck.	
2. Mei		
3. Lisa		
4. Bob		

✔

How many questions did you ask your partner?

☐ 1 ☐ 2 ☐ 3 ☐ 4

How many questions did you answer?

☐ 1 ☐ 2 ☐ 3 ☐ 4

✔ LEARNING LOG

I know these words:

- ☐ ankle
- ☐ arm
- ☐ aspirin
- ☐ back
- ☐ backache
- ☐ bandage
- ☐ bleed
- ☐ breathe
- ☐ chest
- ☐ choke
- ☐ cough
- ☐ cough medicine

- ☐ drink
- ☐ dry
- ☐ ear
- ☐ earache
- ☐ ear drops
- ☐ elbow
- ☐ emergency entrance
- ☐ eye
- ☐ feet
- ☐ fever
- ☐ finger

- ☐ flammable
- ☐ foot
- ☐ gallon
- ☐ hand
- ☐ head
- ☐ headache
- ☐ heart attack
- ☐ heat
- ☐ internally
- ☐ knee
- ☐ leg
- ☐ liquids

- ☐ lobby
- ☐ main entrance
- ☐ mouth
- ☐ neck
- ☐ nose
- ☐ out of reach
- ☐ pint
- ☐ poison
- ☐ pregnant
- ☐ quart
- ☐ rest
- ☐ runny nose

- ☐ shoulder
- ☐ soft food
- ☐ sore
- ☐ stomach
- ☐ stomachache
- ☐ throat
- ☐ toe
- ☐ visitors' lounge
- ☐ wrist

I can ask:

- ☐ What's the problem?
- ☐ Can you touch your toes?
- ☐ Are you drinking liquids?

I can say:

- ☐ My knee hurts.
- ☐ Yes, I can.
- ☐ No, I can't.
- ☐ You should go to the doctor.
- ☐ You shouldn't put heat on it.

I can write:

- ☐ advice using *should* or *shouldn't*

Spotlight: Writing

1 Read paragraphs A and B below. Find these words. Then answer the question at the end of each paragraph.

Find these words with *S*.
s _h_ _o_ _u_ _l_ _d_
s __ __
s __ __ __ __ __ ' __
s __ __ __
s __ __ __ __

Find these words with *C*.
c _a_ _r_ _e_
c __ __ __ __ __ __ __ __ __
c __ __ __ __ __ __
c __ __ __ __ __ __ __ __
c __ __

OPINION POLLS

A

Should the government provide free hospital care? I asked ten classmates this question. Four classmates think the government should provide free hospital care. Six classmates think the government shouldn't provide free hospital care. In my opinion, the government should provide free hospital care. All sick people need help. What do you think?

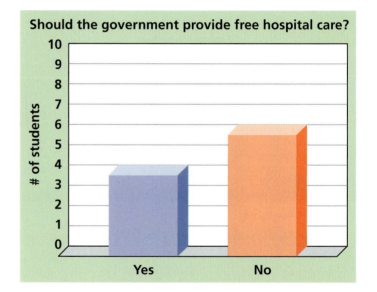

B

Should parents choose a wife for their sons? I asked ten classmates this question. Three classmates think parents should choose their sons' wives.* Seven classmates think sons should choose their wives. In my opinion, parents should choose a wife for their sons. Parents understand their children. They can make good decisions. What do you think?

*Note: The plural of *wife* is *wives*.

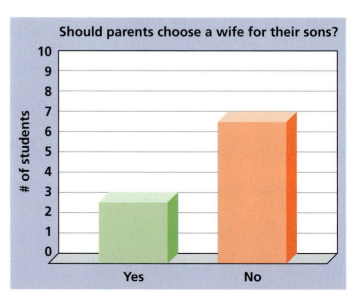

2 Write this paragraph again. Use a piece of paper. Indent the first sentence.

    Should children work outside the home? I asked ten classmates this question. Eight classmates think children shouldn't work. Two classmates think children should work. In my opinion, children shouldn't work. They should study. What do you think?

FOCUS ON WRITING: Indent a Paragraph

Indent the first sentence in a paragraph.
EXAMPLE:

➡️ My name is Ann. I like to watch TV, read books, and go to school. I don't like to go to the supermarket.

3 Choose 1 opinion question. Interview 10 people. Draw a bar graph. Write the results of your opinion poll. Remember to indent.

Opinion Questions

• Should schools provide free lunches?

• Should schools provide computers to all students?

131

LESSON 1

Their new house has 3 bedrooms.

THINGS TO DO

1 Learn New Words 🎧

Look at the pictures. Listen to the words. Then listen and repeat.

①	sofa	⑦	sink	⑬	closet
②	bookcase	⑧	shower	⑭	refrigerator
③	lamp	⑨	toilet	⑮	stove
④	smoke alarm	⑩	bathtub	⑯	dresser
⑤	carpet	⑪	drawer	⑰	bed
⑥	mirror	⑫	cabinet		

2 Write

Write about the pictures.

1. There are _____closets_____ in the kitchen and the bedroom.

2. There is a _____ in the _____ next to the dresser.

3. The refrigerator is in the _____ next to the _____.

4. There are sinks in the _____ and the _____.

5. There are bookcases in the _____ and the _____.

★ ★

TRY THIS Choose a room in your home. List 4 things in it.

EXAMPLE:
Room: bedroom
Things: 3 beds, dresser, lamp, bookcase

Write about the room. Then read your sentences to the class. Your classmates can guess the room.

EXAMPLE: There is a dresser, a lamp, and a bookcase in this room. There are also 3 beds.

★ ★

Living room

Dining room

Bathroom

Kitchen

Bedroom

WINDOW ON GRAMMAR
Comparing Past and Present

A Read the sentences.

PAST	PRESENT
Our old house **had** a bathtub.	Our new house **has** a shower.
Our old house **was** small.	Our new house **is** big.

B Complete the sentences with *has* or *had*.

1. My new house _____ three bedrooms.

2. My old house _____ two bedrooms.

3. She _____ a one-bedroom house last year.

4. This year she _____ a two-bedroom house.

C Complete the sentences with *is* or *was*.

1. My brother _____ in the United States last year.

2. This year he _____ in Mexico.

133

2
LESSON

The Lees' old house had a garage.

THINGS TO DO

1 Learn New Words 🎧

Look at the pictures. Listen to the words. Then listen and repeat.

① pool ④ carport ⑦ porch
② patio ⑤ driveway ⑧ backyard
③ front yard ⑥ garage ⑨ garden

2 Talk About the Pictures

Write 5 sentences about each picture. Share your ideas with a partner.

> EXAMPLES: Picture A
> Dave and Lucy are playing basketball.
>
> Picture B
> The Lees' old house had a garden.

3 Compare

Make a diagram like this. Add 3 things to each part of the diagram. Then share ideas with your class.

The Lees' new house has
a pool

Both houses have
a driveway

The Lees' old house had
a garage

Which house do you like? Why?

★ ★

TRY THIS Describe your dream house. Write 4 sentences. Then tell a partner.

> EXAMPLE: My dream house has. . . .
>
> It doesn't have. . . .

★ ★

Picture B: The Lees' Old House

Picture A:
The Lees' New House

3 LESSON

He fell down the stairs.

THINGS TO DO

1 Learn New Words 🎧

Look at the pictures. Listen to the words. Then listen and repeat.

1. fell down the stairs
2. fell off a ladder
3. fell off a chair
4. slipped in the shower
5. cut his hand with a knife
6. tripped on the carpet

Write the words under the pictures.

2 Practice the Conversation

Listen to the conversation. Then listen and repeat.

A: What happened to Joe?
B: He fell down the stairs.
A: Is he okay now?
B: Yes, I think so.

Work with a partner. Ask about the people in the pictures.

| 1 Mike | 2 Nick | 3 Carol | 4 Donna |

3 Read

Read the bar graph. Answer the questions.

QUESTIONS	ANSWERS
1. How many people got hurt when they fell down the stairs in 2000?	1,050,000
2. How many people got hurt with knives?	_____
3. How many people got hurt when they fell off chairs?	_____
4. How many people got hurt when they tripped on a carpet?	_____

What happened to Joe?

① He _____ .

What happened to Sylvia?

② She _____ .

What happened to Carol?

③ She _____ .

What happened to Mike?

What happened to Nick?

4 He _____ .

1,050,000

Accidents at Home

INJURIES IN THE U.S. IN ONE YEAR

450,000

275,000

150,000

115,000

80,000

STAIRS   KNIVES   CHAIRS   SHOWERS   LADDERS   CARPETS

CAUSES OF INJURIES

The Amazing Almanac, Blackbirch Press (Woodbridge, CT © 2000)

5 He _____ .

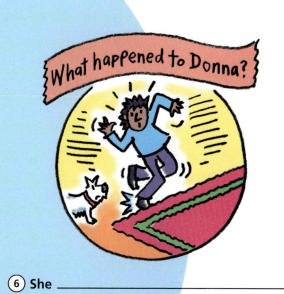

What happened to Donna?

6 She _____

WINDOW ON GRAMMAR
Simple Past: Regular and Irregular Verbs

 A Read the sentences.

REGULAR VERBS

Base Form	Past Form	Examples
like	lik**ed**	I lik**ed** my old house.
work	work**ed**	I work**ed** here last year.

IRREGULAR VERBS

Base Form	Past Form	Examples
fall	**fell**	He **fell** down yesterday.
get	**got**	She **got** hurt last week.
cut	**cut**	I **cut** my hand last night.
go	**went**	I **went** home last year.

B Complete the sentences with the past form of the verb.

1. They _____ their old house.
   (like)

2. Joan _____ down the stairs yesterday.
   (fall)

3. She _____ in a hospital in 2003.
   (work)

4. I _____ to Mexico last month.
   (go)

5. He _____ a good job last week.
   (get)

137

4 LESSON

Housing Ads

THINGS TO DO

1 Learn New Words 🎧

Look at the pictures. Listen to the words. Then listen and repeat.

① **apartment**　② **condo**　③ **mobile home**

2 Write 🎧

Read and listen to the classified ads. Find and write the abbreviations for these words.

WORD	ABBREVIATION(S)
1. apartment	*apt*
2. bathroom	_____
3. bedroom	_____
4. near	_____
5. month	_____
6. garage	_____

3 Read

Read the ads. Answer the questions. Write the letters of the ads.

1. Which places are near schools?　Ad: _a, g_

2. Which places rent for under $900.00?　Ad: _____

3. Which place costs the most money?　Ad: _____

4. Which places have patios?　Ad: _____

5. Which place is interesting to you?
   Why?　Ad: _____

_____

★ ★

TRY THIS Write a classified ad for your dream house.

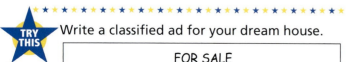

FOR SALE
3 bed, 2 bath, . . .

★ ★

a
House for Rent
3 bed/2 bath
nr schools
patio and pool
$1350/mo
Call Eileen at
555–4000

b
For Rent
Mobile Home
1 bed, 1 bath
Nr public pool
$795/mo
Call Joe 555–1928

c
House for Sale
3BR, 2BA, big kitchen, 2 fireplaces, patio, gar, $210,000
Call Marlene 555–1200, ext. 15

d
FOR RENT
2 Br, 2 BA apt.
pool & patio
$950
call John
555–4583

e
FOR SALE
2 bed, 1.5 bath condo
nr stores
$175,000
Call Smith Realty 555–6767

REALTY

C6

SHOWCASE

f Apartment for Rent

1 bed, 1 bath
$825/mo
Call 555-9904

g Condo for Rent

2 bed, 1 bath,
gar, nr schools
$1100/mo
Call Bev 555-4954

h Mobile Home for Rent

2 bed, 1 bth,
patio, no pets
$875/month
call 555-9948

WINDOW ON GRAMMAR
Simple Past Statements: Negative and Affirmative

★ **A** Read the sentences.

> I **didn't rent** a condo last year. I **rented** a house.
> They **didn't buy** a house in 2001. They **bought** a condo.
> He **didn't hurt** his hand yesterday. He **hurt** his foot.
> She **didn't go** to Miami last week. She **went** to L.A.

★ **B** Complete the sentences.

1. They _____*didn't rent*_____ a house last year. They
   <u>rented</u> a condo.

2. Joan _____ down the stairs last week.
   She <u>fell</u> off a ladder.

3. Bob _____ the mobile home. He <u>liked</u>
   the apartment.

4. I _____ my hand. I <u>hurt</u> my foot.

I'm calling about the house.

1 Practice the Conversation: Calling about a House

Listen to the conversation. Then listen and repeat.

A: I'm calling about the house for rent. Is it still available?

B: Yes, it is.

A: Can you tell me, does it have a front yard?

B: Yes, it does.

Practice the conversation with a partner.
Use these items.

 1 apartment / a garden

 2 condo / a patio

 3 mobile home/ a dining room

 4 house / a pool

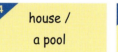 5

2 Practice the Conversation: Asking about Rooms

Listen to the conversation. Then listen and repeat.

A: How many bedrooms does it have?

B: Three.

A: And how many bathrooms?

B: Two.

Practice the conversation with a partner.
Use these items.

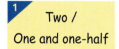 1 Two / One and one-half

 2 One / One

 3 Two small ones / One

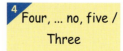 4 Four, ... no, five / Three

 5

3 Practice the Conversation: Asking about Rent

Listen to the conversation. Then listen and repeat.

A: How much is the rent?

B: $1,200.00 a month.

A: Does it include utilities?

B: No, it doesn't.

Practice the conversation with a partner.
Use these items.

1	2	3	4	5
$950.00	$825.00	$400.00	$2,200.00	

WINDOW ON PRONUNCIATION
Stress in Compound Nouns

A Listen to the words. Then listen and repeat.

1. bookcase   3. bedroom   5. bathroom   7. bathtub   9. mailbox
2. carport   4. fireplace   6. grandson   8. drugstore   10. headache

Underline the part of the word that is stressed. For example: bookcase.

B Work with a partner. Ask and answer the questions. Use the words in Activity A.

1. Where can you mail letters?

2. Where can you buy medicine?

3. Where do you sleep?

4. Where do you take a shower?

5. Where can you put books?

6. Who is your daughter's son?

7. If your head hurts, what do you have?

8. Where do you put your car?

9. Where do you take a bath?

10. Where do you make a fire in your home?

UNIT 9: House and Home

Paying Bills

1 Learn New Words 🎧

Look at the bills below. Listen to the words. Then listen and repeat.

① account number
② amount due
③ amount enclosed
④ new charges

SOUTHERN GAS and ELECTRIC COMPANY
P.O. Box 4157
Long Beach, CA 90807-4157

John Alvarez
1622 Walnut Ave.
Long Beach, CA 90807

FOR SERVICES PROVIDED TO:
6464560483-0
1622 Walnut Ave.

Energy Statement

ACCOUNT NUMBER	DUE DATE
6464560483-0	02/07/05

AMOUNT DUE
$ 133.19

Bill Date 01/12/05

Previous Balance $ 132.22
Payment $ 132.22
Balance forward $ 0.00

AMOUNT ENCLOSED
$133.19

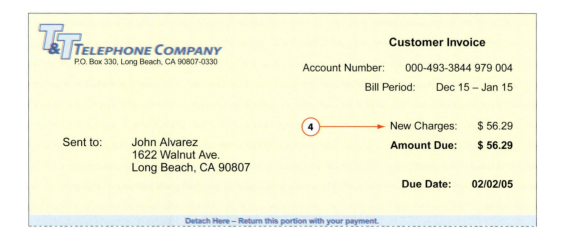

T&T TELEPHONE COMPANY
P.O. Box 330, Long Beach, CA 90807-0330

Customer Invoice

Account Number: 000-493-3844 979 004
Bill Period: Dec 15 – Jan 15

Sent to: John Alvarez
1622 Walnut Ave.
Long Beach, CA 90807

New Charges: $ 56.29
Amount Due: $ 56.29

Due Date: 02/02/05

Detach Here – Return this portion with your payment.

142

2 Read

Read the sentences below. Check (✔) True or False.

		True	False
1.	John's account number with the gas and electric company is 000-493-3844 979 004.	☐	☐
2.	John is paying the gas and electric company $133.19.	☐	☐
3.	John's phone bill is for one month.	☐	☐
4.	John's account number with the telephone company is 000-493-3844 979 004.	☐	☐
5.	The due date for the telephone bill is February 5.	☐	☐

3 Write

Complete the checks. Use the bills from Activity 1.

JOHN ALVAREZ
1622 Walnut Ave.
Long Beach, CA 90807

1129

DATE _____

PAY TO THE
ORDER OF _Southern Gas and Electric Company_ $ ☐

_____ DOLLARS

FIRST NATIONAL BANK of CALIFORNIA
Los Angeles, California

MEMO_____

⑆012345678⑆ 123⑈456 7⑈ 1129

JOHN ALVAREZ
1622 Walnut Ave.
Long Beach, CA 90807

1130

DATE _____

PAY TO THE
ORDER OF_____ $ ☐

_____ DOLLARS

FIRST NATIONAL BANK of CALIFORNIA
Los Angeles, California

MEMO_____

⑆012345678⑆ 123⑈456 7⑈ 1130

7 LESSON

What do you know?

1 Listening Review 🎧

Listen to the conversations. Choose the correct picture. Use the Answer Sheet.

1.

A

B

C

2.

A

B

C

3.

A

B

C

4.

A

B

C

ANSWER SHEET			
1	A	B	C
2	A	B	C
3	A	B	C
4	A	B	C
5	A	B	C
6	A	B	C
7	A	B	C
8	A	B	C

Listen and choose the best answer. Use the Answer Sheet.

5. A. They're on the table.
   B. It's in the living room.
   C. It's for rent.

6. A. No, it has a shower.
   B. Yes, it has a bathtub.
   C. No, it has a bathtub.

7. A. Yes, they do.
   B. No. We live in a mobile home.
   C. Yes, it is.

8. A. It has a yard.
   B. $500.00
   C. two

2 Conversation Check: Pair Work

Student A: Go to page 168.

Student B: Ask your partner questions to complete this chart.

EXAMPLE: **B:** How many rooms are in the White House?

A: There are 132 rooms in the White House.

The U.S. President lives in the White House.

The White House 1600 Pennsylvania Avenue NW Washington, D.C. 20500			
1. Number of rooms:	*132*	5. Number of elevators:	
2. Number of bathrooms:	35	6. Number of swimming pools:	1
3. Number of doors:		7. Number of movie theaters:	
4. Number of fireplaces:	28	8. Number of windows:	147

✔

How many questions did you ask your partner?	How many questions did you answer?
□ 1 □ 2 □ 3 □ 4	□ 1 □ 2 □ 3 □ 4

✔ LEARNING LOG

I know these words:

- □ accident
- □ account number
- □ amount due
- □ amount enclosed
- □ apartment
- □ backyard
- □ bathroom
- □ bathtub
- □ bed
- □ bedroom
- □ bookcase

- □ cabinet
- □ carpet
- □ carport
- □ closet
- □ condo
- □ cut (his hand) with a knife
- □ dining room
- □ drawer
- □ dresser
- □ driveway

- □ fall
- □ fell
- □ front yard
- □ garage
- □ garden
- □ kitchen
- □ ladder
- □ lamp
- □ living room
- □ mirror
- □ mobile home

- □ new charges
- □ patio
- □ pool
- □ porch
- □ refrigerator
- □ sale
- □ shower
- □ sink
- □ slip
- □ slipped
- □ smoke alarm

- □ sofa
- □ stairs
- □ stove
- □ toilet
- □ trip
- □ tripped

I can ask:

- □ What happened to Joe?
- □ Does it have a yard?
- □ How much is the rent?

I can say:

- □ There is a closet in the room.
- □ Our new house has a bathtub.
- □ Our old house had a shower.
- □ We liked our old house.
- □ We didn't buy a house last year.

I can write:

- □ checks to pay bills

UNIT 9: House and Home

Spotlight: Grammar

SIMPLE PAST STATEMENTS		
REGULAR VERBS	**IRREGULAR VERBS**	**VERB BE**
I / He / She / It / You / We / They **worked** yesterday. **didn't work** last week.	I / He / She / It / You / We / They **went** by plane. **didn't go** by train.	I / He / She / It **was** in class yesterday. **wasn't** at home. You / We / They **were** in class yesterday. **weren't** at home.

1 Write about yesterday.

1. She has shrimp for dinner every day.
   She had shrimp for dinner _____ yesterday.

2. He buys a pint of milk every day.
   _____ yesterday.

3. I make the beds every day.
   _____ yesterday.

4. My friends are here every day.
   _____ yesterday.

5. The weather is terrible every day.
   _____ yesterday.

6. He eats six servings of vegetables every day.
   _____ yesterday.

7. I get up before 7:00 every day.
   _____ yesterday.

8. I run to the bus stop every day.
   _____ yesterday.

IRREGULAR VERBS

buy	bought
come	came
cost	cost
drink	drank
get up	got up
go	went
have	had
hurt	hurt
is / are	was / were
eat	ate
leave	left
make	made
meet	met
run	ran
see	saw
sleep	slept
spend	spent

2 Write 5 sentences about what you did yesterday. Use the words in the box.

got up	ate	went	saw
didn't go	was	had	slept

146

INFORMATION QUESTIONS WITH THE SIMPLE PAST

What	**did**	you eat for breakfast?
Where	**did**	we meet them?
When	**did**	they leave for work?
Why	**did**	she leave yesterday?
Who	**did**	he meet at the party?
How much bread	**did**	your children eat yesterday?
How many apples	**did**	they eat yesterday?

3 Match the questions and answers. Then practice with a partner.

1. _e_ Where did you go yesterday?
2. ___ What did you eat this morning?
3. ___ How many glasses of water did you drink yesterday?
4. ___ How many hours did you sleep last night?
5. ___ How much money did you spend yesterday?
6. ___ Who did you dance with last?
7. ___ Who did you call on the telephone yesterday?
8. ___ When did you leave your house this morning?

a. I called my daughter.
b. I left at 8:00.
c. I slept five hours.
d. I ate a banana.
e. I went to work.
f. I drank eight glasses of water.
g. I spent $10.00.
h. I danced with my wife.

4 Complete the conversations. Then practice with a partner.

1. A: Where _____ _did_ _____ you go yesterday?
   B: I _____ to the movies.

2. A: What movie _____ you see?
   B: I _____ a new Chinese movie.

3. A: Did you like it?
   B: Yes, I did. I _____ it a lot.

4. A: What _____ you eat yesterday?
   B: I _____ a lot of fruits and vegetables.

5. A: _____ you eat any meat?
   B: No, I _____.

6. A: Did you buy anything yesterday?
   B: Yes, I did. I _____ a new sweater.

7. A: How much _____ it cost?
   B: It _____ $25.00.

LESSON 1

Can you use a computer?

THINGS TO DO

1 Learn New Words 🎧

Look at the pictures. Listen to the words. Then listen and repeat.

1. chef
2. office manager
3. plumber
4. stylist
5. child care worker
6. mechanic
7. mover
8. construction worker
9. truck driver
10. landscaper

Write the words above the pictures.

2 Write

Write 5 sentences about your friends and family.

> **EXAMPLES:** My husband can lift heavy things.
> My friend Jose can drive a truck.

Read your sentences to the class.

3 Find Someone Who

Talk to your classmates. Find someone who can do each thing. Write the person's name.

A: Can you drive a car ?

B: Yes, I can. / No, I can't.

FIND SOMEONE WHO CAN:	NAME
drive a car	_____
cook rice	_____
lift 50 pounds	_____
use a computer	_____
repair toilets	_____
build a table	_____

Indoor Jobs

1. A _____ cooks food.

2. An _____ _____ uses a computer.

3. A _____ repairs sinks and toilets.

4. A _____ cuts hair.

148

Outdoor Jobs

⑤ A _____

_____

takes care of children.

⑧ A _____

builds buildings.

Indoor/ Outdoor Jobs

⑥ A _____

fixes cars.

⑦ A _____

lifts heavy things.

⑨ A _____

drives a truck.

⑩ A _____

takes care of plants.

WINDOW ON GRAMMAR
Yes/No Questions + Simple Past

⭐**A** Read the questions and answers.

QUESTIONS	ANSWERS
Did you work last week?	**Yes, I did.**
Did you drive a car last week?	**No, I didn't.**

⭐**B** Ask a partner these questions.

1. Did you cook dinner last week?
2. Did you use a computer last month?
3. Did you build furniture last year?
4. Did you drive a truck yesterday?

⭐**C** Write your own question. Then ask a partner.

Did you

_____ ?

149

LESSON 2

Do you have experience?

THINGS TO DO

1 Read

Read the job ads. Take notes in the chart below.

JOB	PART-TIME OR FULL-TIME?	BENEFITS?
Office manager	*full-time*	yes
Construction worker		
Chef		
Child care worker		
Landscaper		
Pharmacist's assistant		

2 Write

Which job do you like? Why? Write 2 sentences. Then tell a partner.

> EXAMPLE: I like the chef job. I like to cook.

3 Practice the Conversation 🎧

Listen to the conversation. Then listen and repeat.

A: I'm calling about the ad for an office manager .

B: Do you have experience?

A: Yes, I do. I have 2 years of experience.

B: Good! Can you come in for an interview tomorrow at 3:00 ?

A: Yes. I'll be there.

Practice the conversation with a partner. Use these items.

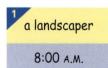

1 a landscaper

8:00 A.M.

2 a child care worker

noon

3 a stylist

7:30 P.M.

4 a truck driver

9:00 in the morning

★★★★★★★★★★★★★★★★★★★★★★★★★★★★★★★★★

TRY THIS Write a help wanted ad for your dream job. Read the ad to your classmates.

★★★★★★★★★★★★★★★★★★★★★★★★★★★★★★★★★

1

Competitive Wages & Benefits Plenty of Work

CONSTRUCTION WORKERS NEEDED
Call 860–555–3209 and leave message. Full-time work.

4

Full-Time Help Wanted Reliable LANDSCAPERS Needed.
• Excellent Pay
• Good Benefits
Apply in Person **Spring Look Landscaping** 66 River Road Santa Anita

2

Legends Grill
Immediate Opening
for Chef
Excellent benefits
Call John for an
Interview
4 Corey Drive
212–555–6948

3

SPS, Inc.
Has an immediate
opening for a
full-time Office
Manager. Benefits
include medical
insurance and paid
vacation. If interested
call for an interview.
(503)555–9438

5

**Child Care Worker
Part-Time**
Flexible hours.
Sorry, no
benefits.
Call Judy Eno
818–555–9483

6

Allen's Drugstore
Pharmacist's assistant
needed. 40 hours a
week. Good benefits.
Call 430–555–3482 for
an interview.

WINDOW ON MATH
Word Problems

 Work with a partner. Answer these word problems.

1. Sam worked 40 hours a week as a mechanic last month. He earned $20.00 an hour. How much did he earn last month?

2. Taka earns $12.00 an hour as a child care worker. She works Monday, Wednesday, and Friday from 7 A.M. to 4 P.M. How much does she earn a week?

3. Robert is a chef's assistant. He works part-time in two restaurants. He works from 7 A.M. to 1 P.M. Monday through Friday and earns $10.00 an hour. He works from 4 P.M. to 11 P.M. on Saturday and Sunday and earns $15.00 an hour. How much does he earn a week?

LESSON 3

Tell me about yourself.

ANNUAL JOB FAIR

THINGS TO DO

1 Talk About the Picture

Write 5 things about the picture.

> EXAMPLES: People are talking.
> The man in the yellow shorts has a dog.

Share your ideas with the class.

2 Listen and Take Notes 🎧

Listen to Rosa's job interview. Write the missing information.

Rosa Perez		
Employer	Job Title	Dates
Lane's	_____	2000 – Present
Lane's	_____	1998 – 2000
The Elephant's Trunk	Salesclerk	_____ – _____

3 Give Opinions

What should you do at a job interview? What shouldn't you do? Make a chart like the one below. Use these ideas. Then add 5 of your own.

be late	dress neatly	chew gum
listen carefully	ask questions	shake hands

AT A JOB INTERVIEW:	
You should . . .	You shouldn't . . .
dress neatly	*be late*

LESSON 4

UNIT 10: Work

The Amazing Story of Mr. Kazi

THINGS TO DO

1 Talk About the Pictures

Write 1 sentence about each picture.

> EXAMPLE: The men are cleaning the car in picture 1.

Share your ideas with the class.

2 Read

Read the story. Put the events in order from first (1) to last (6).

_____ He sold 1 restaurant and bought 3 more.

_____ He worked as a chef's assistant.

_____ He managed a fast-food restaurant.

_____ He owns 168 restaurants.

__1__ Mr. Kazi worked at a car rental company.

_____ He bought a fast-food restaurant.

3 Check True or False

Read the sentences below. Check (✔) True or False.

	True	False
1. Mr. Kazi owned a car rental company.	❐	❐
2. He worked full-time as a chef's assistant.	❐	❐
3. Mr. Kazi was a hard worker.	❐	❐
4. Mr. Kazi borrowed money to buy a restaurant.	❐	❐
5. He was born in the U.S.	❐	❐
6. Today he owns many restaurants.	❐	❐

★★★★★★★★★★★★★★★★★★★★★★★★★★★★★★★★

TRY THIS Write your story. Write about 5 events in your life. Write the events in order from first to last.

★★★★★★★★★★★★★★★★★★★★★★★★★★★★★★★★

1.
Mr. Kazi came to the United States when he was 23 years old. His first job was for a car rental company.

4.
A few years later Mr. Kazi borrowed money from a bank. He bought a fast-food restaurant in very bad condition. He repaired the building and improved the food. He worked seven days a week. Soon the restaurant was making money.

154

2.
On weekends, Mr. Kazi worked as a chef's assistant at a fast-food restaurant. He cleaned the kitchen and helped the chef.

3.
Mr. Kazi worked very hard in the restaurant. Soon the owners of the restaurant promoted him to restaurant manager. He managed the restaurant for the next three years.

5.
A year later Mr. Kazi sold his restaurant. With the money he earned, he bought three more restaurants.

6.
Today Mr. Kazi is the owner of 168 restaurants. He is going to buy more restaurants in the future.

WINDOW ON GRAMMAR
Future with *Be going to*

A Read the sentences.

I	**am going to** look for a new job.
He She It	**is going to** be in Mexico next year.
We They	**are going to** open a restaurant next month.

B Complete the sentences.

1. Mr. Kazi ____*is going to buy*____ more restaurants next year.
(buy)

2. I _____ to Mexico next year.
(go)

3. They _____ medicine next year.
(study)

4. She _____ the restaurant next week.
(manage)

5. We _____ after school next year.
(work)

155

Why did you leave your last job?

LESSON 5

1 Practice the Conversation: Talking about Work Experience 🎧

Listen to the conversation. Then listen and repeat.

A: Tell me about your last job.

B: Well, I worked at a department store .
   I was a salesclerk .

A: Did you like the job?

B: Yes. I liked helping people .
   And there was always something to do.

Practice the conversation with a partner.
Use these items.

1 restaurant /
chef's assistant /
cooking good food

2 school /
child care worker /
taking care of
children

3 salon /
stylist /
cutting hair

4

2 Practice the Conversation: Talking about Changing Jobs 🎧

Listen to the conversation. Then listen and repeat.

A: Why did you leave your last job?

B: I went back to school.

A: I see. And why do you want to work here?

B: I think it's a very good company .

Practice the conversation with a partner.
Use these items.

1 The restaurant
closed. /
restaurant

2 My family
moved here. /
school

3 I didn't have
benefits. /
salon

4

156

3 Practice the Conversation: Answering Job Interview Questions 🎧

Listen to the conversation. Then listen and repeat.

A: Why should I hire you?

B: I'm good with people.

A: That's good. We like our employees to be good with people .

B: I'm glad to hear that.

Practice the conversation with a partner.
Use these items.

1 I work hard.

work hard

2 I have experience.

have experience

3 I listen carefully.

listen carefully

4

WINDOW ON PRONUNCIATION 🎧
Stressing Important Words in Sentences

A Listen to the sentences. Then listen and repeat.

1. Tell me about your last <u>job</u>.

2. I worked at a department store.

3. Why did you leave your last job?

4. Why should I hire you?

Underline the stressed words.

B Listen to the questions. Underline the stressed words.

1. A: What did you do in your last job?

   B: _____

2. A: Did you like the job?

   B: _____

3. A: Why should I hire you?

   B: _____

4. A: Why do you want to work here?

   B: _____

Work with a partner. Ask and answer the questions.

Job Applications

1 Read

Read about Francis Yasine. Then complete the job application below for Francis.

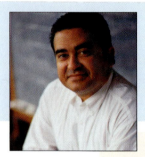

My name is Francis Martin Yasine, and I live at 2435 Melford Avenue in Sacramento, California. In my country, I worked as a mechanic. I liked my job a lot. My friends say I'm a good mechanic. Now I don't have a job. I really want a full-time job.

Job Application
Personal Information

First Name: _____

Middle Initial: _____

Last Name: _____

Birth Date: __6__ / __23__ / __70__

Present Address: _____

City: _____

State: _____

Zip Code: _95652_____

Phone Number: _(916) 555-4938_____

* Are you currently employed?　　　　☐ Yes　　☐ No

* Do you have a valid driver's license?　☑ Yes　　☐ No

* Do you have access to an automobile?　☑ Yes　　☐ No

* Number of hours/week desired: _____

* Days and A.M./P.M. hours available:

	Mon.	Tues.	Wed.	Thurs.	Fri.	Sat.	Sun.
A.M.	☑	☑	☑	☑	☑	☑	☐
P.M.	☑	☑	☑	☑	☑	☐	☐

2 Write

Complete this job application with information about yourself.

Job Application
Personal Information

First Name: _____

Middle Initial: _____

Last Name: _____

Birth Date: _____ / _____ / _____

Present Address: _____

City: _____

State: _____

Zip Code: _____

Phone Number: _____

* Are you currently employed?   ☐ Yes   ☐ No

* Do you have a valid driver's license?   ☐ Yes   ☐ No

* Do you have access to an automobile?   ☐ Yes   ☐ No

* Number of hours/week desired: _____

* Days and A.M./ P.M. hours available:

	Mon.	Tues.	Wed.	Thurs.	Fri.	Sat.	Sun.
A.M.	☐	☐	☐	☐	☐	☐	☐
P.M.	☐	☐	☐	☐	☐	☐	☐

3 Interview

Work with a partner. Ask your partner 5 questions about his or her job application.

EXAMPLE: A: Do you have a valid driver's license?
          B: Yes, I do. / No, I don't.

7
LESSON

What do you know?

1 Listening Review 🎧

Listen and choose the correct answer. Use the Answer Sheet.

1. A. They fix cars.
   B. They cut hair.
   C. They take care of children.

2. A. Yes, he can.
   B. No, they can't.
   C. No, he's not.

3. A. Yes, she does.
   B. Yes, she can.
   C. Yes, she did.

4. A. Yes, it is.
   B. Yes, they did.
   C. Yes, she is.

5. A. I worked at a restaurant.
   B. My family moved.
   C. I liked it very much.

6. A. I work very hard.
   B. You shouldn't be late.
   C. Yes, you should.

7. A. $20.00
   B. $200.00
   C. $2,000.00

8. A. $400.00
   B. $800.00
   C. $1,000.00

ANSWER SHEET			
1	Ⓐ	Ⓑ	Ⓒ
2	Ⓐ	Ⓑ	Ⓒ
3	Ⓐ	Ⓑ	Ⓒ
4	Ⓐ	Ⓑ	Ⓒ
5	Ⓐ	Ⓑ	Ⓒ
6	Ⓐ	Ⓑ	Ⓒ
7	Ⓐ	Ⓑ	Ⓒ
8	Ⓐ	Ⓑ	Ⓒ

2 Dictation 🎧

Listen and write the questions you hear.

1. _____

2. _____

3. _____

Answer the questions you wrote above.

1. _____

2. _____

3. _____

3 Conversation Check: Pair Work

Student A: Go to page 168.

Student B: Ask your partner questions about Jane Roe. Answer your partner's questions about Bob Wu.

EXAMPLE:
B: When did Jane work at Lane's Department Store?
A: From March 1998 to May 2000.

Jane Roe
1234 Altadena Drive
Altadena, California 91001
626-555-3954   jroe@dayna.net

Work Background

5/2000 to present	*Store Manager*	**Gould's Drugstore**
(3/1998) to 5/2000	*Assistant Manager*	**Lane's Department Store**
7/1995 to 12/1997	( )	**Regina's Boutique**
( )	( )	**Westville Public Library**

Bob Wu
5395 Manchester Road
Andover, Illinois 61233
309-555-4503   bbwu@access.net

Work Background

7/2002 to present	*Construction Worker*	**ABC Industries**
9/1995 to 6/2002	*Truck Driver*	**HFC Inc.**
3/1993 to 3/1995	*Landscaper*	**Greenthumbs**
11/1991 to 1/1993	*Cashier*	**Sam's Supermarket**

How many questions did you ask your partner?	How many questions did you answer?
□ 1 □ 2 □ 3 □ 4	□ 1 □ 2 □ 3 □ 4

✔ LEARNING LOG

I know these words:

- □ ask questions
- □ be late
- □ benefits
- □ build
- □ chef
- □ chew gum
- □ child care worker
- □ construction worker
- □ cook
- □ dress neatly
- □ drive
- □ heavy
- □ indoor
- □ landscaper
- □ lift
- □ listen carefully
- □ make
- □ mechanic
- □ mover
- □ office manager
- □ outdoor
- □ plumber
- □ reliable
- □ repair
- □ shake hands
- □ stylist
- □ take care of
- □ truck driver

I can ask:
- □ Can you use a computer?
- □ Did you work last week?
- □ Do you have experience?
- □ Did you like the job?
- □ Why did you leave your last job?

I can say:
- □ Yes, I did.
- □ No, I didn't.
- □ You shouldn't be late.
- □ I'm going to look for a new job.

I can write:
- □ a job application

Spotlight: Writing

1 Read the stories below. Find these words.

Find these words with H.
h _a_ _p_ _p_ _e_ _n_ _e_ _d_
h __ __
h __ __ __
h __ __ __ __ __
h __ ' __
h __ __ __ __ __ __
h __ __ __ __
h __ __ __ __

Find these words with M.
m _e_
M __
m __ __ __ __
m __ __ __ __ __
M __ __ __ __

STORIES 🎧

Victor

Last week was a good week for me. Two good things happened. I got a new job and we bought a new TV. Only one bad thing happened. My daughter fell down and cut her hand. She's okay now.

Angela

Last week was pretty good for me. Three good things happened. I bought a new dress and I went to a movie. I also got a new cell phone. Nothing bad happened last week.

Amy

Last week wasn't very good for me. One bad thing happened. My husband got sick. Now he's in the hospital. Two good things happened, too. My friends came to my house and helped me. My mother also came from Miami. She is taking care of my children.

2 Complete the paragraph below. Use the information in the Idea List.

IDEA LIST	
Good Things	**Bad Things**
I earned some money.	I had a problem at work.
I ate at a good restaurant.	I got a parking ticket.
I sold my car.	I had a headache for two days.

FOCUS ON WRITING: Idea Lists

Before you write a paragraph, write your ideas in a list. Then write your paragraph.

Last week was pretty good for me. Three good things happened.
I _____earned some money_____ and I _____ .
I also _____ . Three bad things happened.
I _____ and I _____ .
I also _____ .

3 What happened to you last week? Make a list. Then write your paragraph.

IDEA LIST	
Good Things	**Bad Things**

Conversation Checks

Conversation Check: Pair Work

Student A: Ask your partner questions to complete this chart. Write the answers.

EXAMPLE: **A:** What is Don's occupation?
B: Police Officer

First Name	Last Name	Gender	Occupation	Telephone Number
1. Don	Garcia	M	*Police Officer*	(545) 555–5943
2. Gloria	Ramos	F		(534) 555–6989
3. Van	Pham	F	Doctor	
4. Steve	Smith	M	Cashier	(543) 555–9004
5. Victor		M	Bus driver	

How many questions did you ask your partner?	How many questions did you answer?
☐ 1 ☐ 2 ☐ 3 ☐ 4 ☐ 5	☐ 1 ☐ 2 ☐ 3 ☐ 4 ☐ 5

Conversation Check: Pair Work

Student A: Ask your partner the 2 questions below. Mark the places on the map.

1. Where's the hospital?

2. Where's the school?

How many questions did you ask your partner?	How many questions did you answer?
☐ 1 ☐ 2	☐ 1 ☐ 2

Conversation Check: Pair Work

Student A: Ask your partner questions to complete this chart.

EXAMPLE: **A:** When is the community center open on Sunday?
B: It is closed.

	Sunday	Monday	Tuesday	Wednesday	Thursday	Friday	Saturday
Community Center	closed	closed	noon to 8 P.M.	noon to 8 P.M.	noon to 8 P.M.	noon to 10 P.M.	noon to 10 P.M.
Laundromat	7 A.M. to 10 P.M.		noon to 10 P.M.	10 A.M. to 10 P.M.	10 A.M. to 10 P.M.	10 A.M. to 10 P.M.	7 A.M. to 10 P.M.
Drugstore	noon to 8 P.M.	8 A.M. to 9 P.M.	8 A.M. to 9 P.M.	8 A.M. to 9 P.M.		8 A.M. to 9 P.M.	
Supermarket	8 A.M. to 8 P.M.	6 A.M. to midnight	6 A.M. to midnight		6 A.M. to midnight	6 A.M. to midnight	6 A.M. to 10 P.M.

How many questions did you ask your partner?	How many questions did you answer?
☐ 1 ☐ 2 ☐ 3 ☐ 4 ☐ 5	☐ 1 ☐ 2 ☐ 3 ☐ 4 ☐ 5

Conversation Check: Pair Work

Student A: Answer questions about appointment cards 1 and 2. Ask your partner questions about cards 3 and 4.

EXAMPLE: **A:** When is Lisa's appointment?
B: It's on April 10.
A: What time?

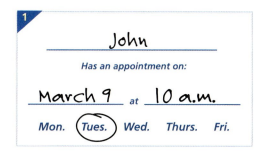

1

John

Has an appointment on:

March 9 *at* 10 a.m.

Mon.   (Tues.)   Wed.   Thurs.   Fri.

2

Name: Sue

Your next appointment is on:

May 16 *at* 4 p.m.

We reserve the right to charge for appointments canceled or broken without 24 hours advance notice.

3

Appointment Card

For: Lisa   M _____   TH _____
On: April 10   T _____   F _____
At: _____   W _____

If unable to keep this appointment, kindly give 24 hours notice.

4

Appointment

For: Paul

_____ @ _____

☑ Mon.   ☐ Tues.   ☐ Wed.   ☐ Thurs.   ☐ Fri.

How many questions did you ask your partner?	How many questions did you answer?
☐ 1 ☐ 2 ☐ 3 ☐ 4 ☐ 5	☐ 1 ☐ 2 ☐ 3 ☐ 4 ☐ 5

5 UNIT Conversation Check: Pair Work

Student A: Ask your partner questions to complete the price tags.

EXAMPLE: **A:** What size is the red sweater?
B: It's a large.
A: How much is it?

a. Size: LARGE
Price:

b. Size: EXTRA LARGE
Price: $50.00

c. Size:
Price:

d. Size: MEDIUM
Price: $48.00

How many questions did you ask your partner?	How many questions did you answer?
☐ 1 ☐ 2 ☐ 3 ☐ 4	☐ 1 ☐ 2 ☐ 3 ☐ 4

✔

 6 UNIT Conversation Check: Pair Work

Student A: Ask your partner questions to complete this chart.

EXAMPLE: **A:** How much is a carton of orange juice?
B: $2.00

	FOOD	PRICE (How much?)	SIZE/AMOUNT (What size?)
1		$2.50	28 ounces
2		$3.00	8 ounces
3		*$2.00*	
4			

How many questions did you ask your partner?	How many questions did you answer?
☐ 1 ☐ 2 ☐ 3 ☐ 4	☐ 1 ☐ 2 ☐ 3 ☐ 4

✔

UNIT 7 Conversation Check: Pair Work

Student A: Ask your partner questions to complete this chart.

EXAMPLE: **A:** Where does John live?
B: He lives in California.

Bob's Family			
Name	Relationship	Where does he/she live?	What does he/she do for fun?
1. John	Bob's father	*California*	takes pictures
2. Cora		Texas	
3. Jodie	Bob's sister		dances
4. Lisa	Bob's wife	Florida	
5. Beth		Texas	
6. Richard	Bob's brother	Florida	plays soccer

How many questions did you ask your partner?	How many questions did you answer?
☐ 1 ☐ 2 ☐ 3 ☐ 4 ☐ 5 ☐ 6 ☐ 7	☐ 1 ☐ 2 ☐ 3 ☐ 4 ☐ 5 ☐ 6 ☐ 7

UNIT 8 Conversation Check: Pair Work

Student A: Ask your partner questions to complete this chart.

EXAMPLE: **A:** What's the matter with Mei?
B: She has a stomachache.
A: What's she doing for it?

Name	What's the matter with him/her?	What's he/she doing for it?
1. Tom		
2. Mei	*She has a stomachache.*	
3. Lisa		
4. Bob		

How many questions did you ask your partner?
☐ 1 ☐ 2 ☐ 3 ☐ 4
How many questions did you answer?
☐ 1 ☐ 2 ☐ 3 ☐ 4

Conversation Check: Pair Work

UNIT 9

Student A: Ask your partner questions to complete this chart.

EXAMPLE: **A:** How many bathrooms are in the White House?
B: There are 35 bathrooms in the White House.

The U.S. President lives in the White House.

The White House
1600 Pennsylvania Avenue NW
Washington, D.C. 20500

1. Number of rooms:	132	5. Number of elevators:	3
2. Number of bathrooms:	35	6. Number of swimming pools:	
3. Number of doors:	412	7. Number of movie theaters:	1
4. Number of fireplaces:		8. Number of windows:	

✔

How many questions did you ask your partner?	How many questions did you answer?
☐ 1 ☐ 2 ☐ 3 ☐ 4	☐ 1 ☐ 2 ☐ 3 ☐ 4

Conversation Check: Pair Work

UNIT 10

Student A: Answer your partner's questions about Jane Roe. Ask your partner questions about Bob Wu.

EXAMPLE: **A:** When did Bob work at HFC Inc.?

B: From September 1995 to June 2002.

Jane Roe
1234 Altadena Drive
Altadena, California 91001
626–555–3954   jroe@dayna.net

Work Background

5/2000 to present	*Store Manager*	**Gould's Drugstore**
3/1998 to 5/2000	*Assistant Manager*	**Lane's Department Store**
7/1995 to 12/1997	*Assistant*	**Regina's Boutique**
9/1993 to 5/1995	*Librarian's Assistant*	**Westville Public Library**

Bob Wu
5395 Manchester Road
Andover, Illinois 61233
309–555–4503   bbwu@access.net

✔

Work Background

7/2002 to present	Construction Worker	**ABC Industries**
9/1995 to 6/2002		**HFC Inc.**
3/1993 to 3/1995		**Greenthumbs**
	Cashier	**Sam's Supermarket**

How many questions did you ask your partner?
☐ 1 ☐ 2 ☐ 3 ☐ 4
How many questions did you answer?
☐ 1 ☐ 2 ☐ 3 ☐ 4

A Present Tense of *Be*

Affirmative Statements

I	am	a student.	We	are	students.
You	are	a student.	You	are	students.
He	is	a student.	They	are	students.
She	is	a student.			
It	is	a book.			

Negative Statements

I	am not	a teacher.	We	are not	teachers.
You	are not	a teacher.	You	are not	teachers.
He	is not	a teacher.	They	are not	teachers.
She	is not	a teacher.			
It	is not	a map.			

Contractions

I am → I'm		I am not → I'm not	
You are → You're		You are not → You aren't/You're not	
He is → He's		He is not → He isn't/He's not	
She is → She's		She is not → She isn't/She's not	
It is → It's		It is not → It isn't/It's not	
We are → We're		We are not → We aren't/We're not	
You are → You're		You are not → You aren't/You're not	
They are → They're		They are not → They aren't/They're not	

Yes/No Questions and Short Answers

Am	I			I	am.		I	'm not.
Are	you			you	are.		you	aren't.
Is	he			he	is.		he	isn't.
Is	she	late?	Yes,	she	is.	No,	she	isn't.
Is	it			it	is.		it	isn't.
Are	we			we	are.		we	aren't.
Are	you			you	are.		you	aren't.
Are	they			they	are.		they	aren't.

Information Questions				
Where	am are is is is are are	I? you? he? she? it? we? they?	Who are you? Who is she?	Why are you here? Why is she here?
			What is your name? What is her name?	How are you? How is she?
			When is the party? When are the holidays?	How old are you? How old is she?

B Possessives

Possessive Nouns
To form the possessive of any singular noun, add an apostrophe and *-s*.   **Examples:**   John's book   Amy's map   the teacher's desk
To form the possessive of a plural noun that ends in *-s*, just add an apostrophe.   **Examples:**   the girls' desks   the boys' room
To form the possessive of a plural noun that does not end in *-s*, add an apostrophe and *-s*.   **Examples:**   the children's teacher   the women's team   the men's room

Possessive Adjectives				
Here is	my your his her its	paper.	Here is	our your their	book.

C There is/There are

Affirmative Statements					
There is	one store a bank a park	on State St.	There are	two restaurants several stores lots of people	on Main St.

Negative Statements

There isn't	a clock in the room. one book here. any paper in my notebook.	There aren't	any books in the room. any cars on the street. any pens by the phone.

Yes/No Questions and Short Answers

Is there	a clock a window a closet	in your room?	Yes, there is. No, there isn't.
Are there	any books pens notebooks	on the table?	Yes, there are. No, there aren't.

D Simple Present Tense

Affirmative Statements

I You He She It	like like likes likes likes	music.	We You They	like like like	music.

Negative Statements

I You He She It	don't like don't like doesn't like doesn't like doesn't like	tea.	We You They	don't like don't like don't like	tea.

Yes/No Questions and Short Answers

Do Do Does Does Does Do Do Do	I you he she it we you they	like milk?	Yes,	I you he she it we you they	do. do. does. does. does. do. do. do.	No,	I you he she it we you they	don't. don't. doesn't. doesn't. doesn't. don't. don't. don't.

Information Questions

Where	do do does does does do do	I you he she it we they	live?	Who do you live with? Who does she live with?	Why do you smoke? Why does she smoke?
				What do you like? What does she like?	How do you do this? How does she do this?
				When do you get up? When does she get up?	How often do you eat? How often does he eat?

E Present Continuous Tense

Affirmative Statements

I	am working.	We	are working.
You	are working.	You	are working.
He	is working.	They	are working.
She	is working.		
It	is working.		

Negative Statements

I	am not working.	We	aren't working.
You	aren't working.	You	aren't working.
He	isn't working.	They	aren't working.
She	isn't working.		
It	isn't working.		

Yes/No Questions and Short Answers

Am	I			I	am.		I	am not.
Are	you			you	are.		you	aren't.
Is	he			he	is.		he	isn't.
Is	she	working?	Yes,	she	is.	No,	she	isn't.
Is	it			it	is.		it	isn't.
Are	we			we	are.		we	aren't.
Are	you			you	are.		you	aren't.
Are	they			they	are.		they	aren't.

Information Questions

What	am are is is is are are	I you he she it we they	doing?		Who are you talking to? Who is she talking to?	Why are you leaving? Why is she leaving?
					Where are you working? Where is she working?	How are you feeling? How is she feeling?

F Simple Past Tense

Affirmative Statements

I You He She It	worked	yesterday.		We You They	worked	yesterday.

Negative Statements

I You He She It	didn't work	yesterday.		We You They	didn't work	yesterday.

Yes/No Questions and Short Answers

Did	I you he she it we you they	work yesterday?		Yes,	I you he she it we you they	did.	No,	I you he she it we you they	didn't.

Information Questions

Where	did	I you he she it we they	work?	Who did you work with? Who did she talk to?	Why did you go? Why did she leave?
				Who worked yesterday? Who called?	How did you get here? How did she feel?
				When did you arrive? When did she call?	What did you do? What did she say?

Past Tense of Irregular Verbs

buy	bought	eat	ate
come	came	leave	left
cost	cost	make	made
do	did	meet	met
drink	drank	pay	paid
get up	got up	run	ran
go	went	see	saw
have	had	sleep	slept
hurt	hurt	spend	spent
is/are	was/were		

G Nouns

Plural Nouns

To form the plural of:		Examples
most nouns	add -s	book—books student—students
most nouns that end in s, sh, ch, x, or z	add -es	dish—dishes couch—couches
most nouns that end in ay, ey, oy, or uy	add -s	boy—boys day—days
most nouns that end in -f or -fe	change -f to -v and add -es or -s	wife—wives loaf—loaves
most nouns that end in a consonant and -y	change the -y to -i and add -es	story—stories candy—candies
most nouns that end in -o	add -s	radio—radios
some nouns that end in consonant and -o	add -es	potato—potatoes

Note: This audio script offers support for many of the activities in the Student Book. When the words on the Student Book page are identical to those on the audio program, the script is not provided here.

UNIT ONE
Lesson 2. (page 6)
1. Learn New Words
Look at the picture. Listen to the words.
Then listen and repeat.

1. teacher	Where's the teacher?
2. wall	What's on the wall?
3. clock	Where's the clock?
4. door	Where's the door?
5. board	Where's the board?
6. table	Where's the table?
7. calendar	Where's the calendar?
8. map	Where's the map?
9. notebook	Where's the notebook?
10. pen	Where's the pen?
11. pencil	Where's the pencil?
12. piece of paper	Where's the piece of paper?
13. book	Where's the book?
14. floor	What's on the floor?
15. chair	Where's the chair?
16. computer	Where's the computer?
17. desk	Where's the desk?
18. student	Where's the student?
19. window	Where's the window?

Lesson 4. (page 10)
1. Learn New Words
Look at the picture. Listen to the information.

His first name is Paul. His middle name is Richard. His last name is Bridges. His address is 8517 Alvarado Street in Los Angeles, California. The zip code is 91012. Paul's telephone number is area code 310-555-5678. His birthplace is Sacramento, California in the United States. His gender is male. His marital status is married. He's a teacher. That's his occupation.

Listen and repeat.

1. middle name	10. gender
2. address	11. male
3. street	12. female
4. city	13. marital status
5. state	14. single
6. zip code	15. married
7. telephone number	16. divorced
8. area code	17. occupation
9. birthplace	

Lesson 5. (page 12)
1. Practice the Conversation: Greeting Someone
Listen to the conversation. Then listen and repeat.

A: Hello. I'm Mr. Campos.
B: Nice to meet you, Mr. Campos. I'm Ms. Jones.
A: Nice to meet you.

Listen to the new words and expressions. Then repeat.

Hi.	How do you do?	Hello.
Mr.	Ms.	Mrs.

Lesson 5. (page 12)
2. Practice the Conversation: Introducing Someone
Listen to the conversation. Then listen and repeat.

A: Hi, Jon. How are you?
B: Fine, thanks. And you?
A: I'm fine. Jon, this is my friend Gina.
B: Hi, Gina. Nice to meet you.

Listen to the new words and expressions. Then repeat.

Good   Not bad   OK   Great
I want to introduce you to Gina.
I want you to meet Gina.
This is Gina.

Lesson 5. (page 13)
3. Practice the Conversation: Saying Good-bye
Listen to the conversation. Then listen and repeat.

A: Good-bye, Jon.
B: Bye, David.
A: You too.

Listen to the new expressions. Then repeat.

Have a nice day.
See you later.
Nice to see you.
Have a great day.
Have a good day.

Lesson 5. (page 13)
Window on Pronunciation
Long Vowel Sounds: *I* and *E*
C. Listen and circle the word you hear.

1. my	my	4. write	write
2. he	he	5. bye	bye
3. E	E	6. we	we

Lesson 6. (page 14)
1. Learn New Words
Look at the pictures below. Listen to the words.
Then listen and repeat.

1. dentist	Joan Baxter is a dentist.
2. bus driver	Larry Fisher is a bus driver.
3. pharmacist	Ken Park is a pharmacist.
4. doctor	Emma Lambert is a doctor.
5. salesclerk	Paul Ming is a salesclerk.
6. machinist	David Campos is a machinist.
7. police officer	Gina Mata is a police officer.
8. nurse	Leo Brunov is a nurse.
9. cashier	Amy Craft is a cashier.

Lesson 7. (page 16)
1. Listening Review
Listen and choose the correct answer.
Use the Answer Sheet below.

1. Open your book.
2. Her book is on the floor.
3. She's a teacher.
4. It's a calendar.
5. What's his telephone number?
6. What's her zip code?
7. What's her occupation?
8. What state is he from?
9. What's their area code?
10. What's her address?

UNIT TWO
Lesson 1. (page 20)
2. Learn New Words
Look at the pictures. Listen to the words.
Then listen and repeat.

1. fire station	Where's the fire station?
2. police station	Where's the police station?
3. post office	Where's the post office?
4. community center	Where's the community center?
5. library	Where's the library?
6. bookmobile	Where's the bookmobile?
7. school	Where's the school?
8. park	Where's the park?
9. bank	Where's the bank?
10. drugstore	Where's the drugstore?
11. gas station	Where's the gas station?
12. supermarket	Where's the supermarket?
13. hospital	Where's the hospital?
14. laundromat	Where's the laundromat?
15. movie theater	Where's the movie theater?
16. restaurant	Where's the restaurant?

Lesson 2. (page 22)
1. Learn New Words
Look at the pictures. Listen to the words.
Then listen and repeat.

1. next to	The post office is next to the drugstore.
2. between	The laundromat is between the drugstore and the supermarket.
3. across from	The bank is across from the post office.
4. in front of	The bookmobile is in front of the library.
5. near	The school is near the park.
6. in back of	There's a park in back of the library.
7. on the corner of	There's a gas station on the corner of State Street and Main Street.

Lesson 3. (page 24)
2. Learn New Words
Look at the picture. Listen to the words.
Then listen and repeat.

1. bus stop	There's a bus stop near the laundromat.
2. parking lot	There's a parking lot next to the supermarket.
3. bus	There's a bus near the bus stop.
4. ambulance	There's an ambulance in front of the hospital.
5. crosswalk	There's a crosswalk near the movie theater.
6. sidewalk	There's a sidewalk in front of the movie theater.
7. mailbox	There's a mailbox in front of the post office.
8. stoplight	There's a stoplight on Main Street.
9. truck	There's a truck on Pine Street.
10. taxi	There's a taxi across from the community center.
11. car	There's a car across from the book mobile.
12. pay phone	There's a pay phone on the corner of Front Street and Main Street.
13. ATM	There's an ATM next to the bank.
14. stop	
15. no parking	
16. do not enter	
17. no right turn	
18. no left turn	
19. one way	

Lesson 4. (page 26)
2. Learn New Words
Look at the map. Listen to the words.
Then listen and repeat.

1. capital	The capital of Florida is Tallahassee.
2. north of	New York is north of Pennsylvania.
3. south of	Texas is south of Oklahoma.
4. east of	Texas is east of New Mexico.
5. west of	Arizona is west of New Mexico.

Lesson 5. (page 28)
1. Practice the Conversation: Asking for Repetition
Listen to the conversation. Then listen and repeat.

A: Is there a restaurant near here?
B: Excuse me?
A: Is there a restaurant near here?
B: Yes, there is. There's one on Pine.
A: Thanks.

Listen to the new expressions. Then repeat.
I'm sorry, what was that?
Please say that again.
What was that?

Lesson 5. (page 28)
2. Practice the Conversation:
Saying You Don't Know
Listen to the conversation. Then listen and repeat.

A: Excuse me. Is there a drugstore near here?
B: I'm not sure.
A: Okay. Thanks anyway.

Listen to the new expressions. Then repeat.

Sorry, I don't know.
Sorry, I'm new in town.
Sorry, I'm not sure.

Lesson 5. (page 29)
3. Practice the Conversation:
Asking a Follow-Up Question
Listen to the conversation. Then listen and repeat.

A: Where's Sacramento?
B: It's in California.
A: In the north or south of the state?
B: In the north.

Listen to the new places. Then repeat.

Atlanta   Tallahassee   Lansing
Georgia   Florida   Michigan

Lesson 6. (page 30)
1. Learn New Words
Look at the pictures. Listen to the words.
Then listen and repeat.

1. librarian   Where's the librarian?
2. checkout desk   Where's the checkout desk?
3. library card   Where's your library card?
4. magazines   Where are the magazines?
5. audiobooks   Where are the audiobooks?
6. videos   Where are the videos?
7. children's books   Where are the children's books?

Lesson 7. (page 32)
1. Listening Review
Listen and choose the correct place.
Use the Answer Sheet.

1. What's next to the gas station?
2. What's across from the police station?
3. What's between the library and the hospital?
4. What's on the corner of Main Street and Pine Street?
5. What's west of the bank?
6. What's north of the supermarket?

Lesson 7. (page 32)
2. Dictation
Listen and write the words you hear.

1.
   A: Excuse me. Where's the post office?
   B: It's on Front Street.

2.
   A: Excuse me. Is there a mailbox near here?
   B: Yes, there is. It's in front of the library.

3.
   A: What's the capital of New Mexico?
   B: I'm not sure.

UNIT THREE
Lesson 1. (page 36)
2. Learn New Words
Look at the pictures. Listen to the words.
Then listen and repeat.
TIMES
1. six o'clock   It's six o'clock.
2. noon   It's noon.
3. midnight   It's midnight.
4. 9:00 A.M.   It's 9:00 P.M.
5. 9:00 P.M.   It's 9:00 A.M.
TIME OF DAY
6. in the morning   It's 8 o'clock in the morning.
7. in the afternoon   It's 2:15 in the afternoon.
8. in the evening   It's 7:30 in the evening.
9. at night   It's 11:45 at night.
OTHER WORDS
10. before   It's ten before 3:00.
11. after   It's ten after 3:00.
12. minutes   It's fifteen minutes after four.

Lesson 3. (page 40)
1. Learn New Words
Look at the pictures. Listen to the words.
Then listen and repeat.

1. penny   A penny equals one cent.
2. nickel   A nickel equals five cents.
3. dime   A dime equals ten cents.
4. quarter   A quarter equals twenty-five cents.
5. half-dollar   A half-dollar equals fifty cents.
6. dollar   How much is the pen? It's a dollar.
7. five dollars   How much is the magazine? It's
                      five dollars.
8. ten dollars   How much is the calendar? It's ten
                      dollars.
9. twenty dollars   How much is the clock? It's twenty
                      dollars.
10. fifty dollars   How much is the chair? It's fifty
                      dollars.
11. one hundred   How much is the table? It's one
    dollars   hundred dollars.
12. one thousand   How much is the computer? It's
    dollars   one thousand dollars.

Lesson 4. (page 42)
1. Learn New Words
Look at the pictures. Listen to the words.
Then listen and repeat.

1. check   It's a check.
2. check number   The check number is one twenty four.
3. amount   The check amount is twelve dollars.
4. signature   It's David's signature.

Lesson 5. (page 44)
1. Practice the Conversation: Asking about Business Hours
Listen to the conversation. Then listen and repeat.

A: Hello. Anderson's Drugstore. Can I help you?
B: Yes. What are your hours on Thursday?
A: We're open from eight to six.
B: Thank you.

Lesson 5. (page 44)
2. Practice the Conversation: Calling Directory Assistance
Listen to the conversation. Then listen and repeat.

A: Welcome to Horizon. What city and state?
B: Miami, Florida.
A: What listing?
B: Rafael Hernandez.
A: The number is area code 305-555-5938.

Listen to the new places. Then repeat.

New York, New York   Houston, Texas
Santa Ana, California   Miami, Florida

Lesson 5. (page 45)
3. Listen and Write: Listening to a Recorded Message
Listen and write the missing numbers.
Then listen and check.

Thank you for calling the Coral Beach Public Library. For hours, press 1.
The library is open Monday through Thursday from eleven to nine. On Friday and Saturday, the library is open from nine to five. Good-bye.

Lesson 5. (page 45)
Window on Pronunciation
***Thirteen* or *Thirty*? Syllable Stress in Numbers**
B. Listen and circle the numbers you hear.

1. 13   5. 17
2. 40   6. 80
3. 50   7. 90
4. 16

C. Listen and point to the numbers you hear.

1. It's six-fifteen.
2. It's fifty cents.
3. From 9:30 A.M. to 6:00 P.M.
4. The price is $3.18.

Lesson 7. (page 48)
1. Listening Review
Listen and choose the time you hear.
Use the Answer Sheet.

1.
   A: Excuse me. What time is it?
   B: It's five o'clock.
   A: Okay. Thanks.

2.
   A: CTS Drugstore.
   B: Yes. When do you open tomorrow?
   A: At 8:00.
   B: Thanks.
3.
   A: When's the next bus?
   B: It's at 8:45.
   A: Thanks.
4.
   A: When's your class today?
   B: It's at noon.
   A: Are you sure?
   B: Yes, of course.

Listen and choose the correct answer.
Use the Answer Sheet.

5. What are your hours on Monday?
6. What time is it?
7. How much is it?
8. When's the party?
9. What day is it?
10. How much is it?

UNIT FOUR
Lesson 1. (page 52)
1. Learn New Words
Look at the pictures. Listen to the words.
Then listen and repeat.

1. January	It's January.
2. February	It's February.
3. March	It's March.
4. April	It's April.
5. May	It's May.
6. June	It's June.
7. July	It's July.
8. August	It's August.
9. September	It's September.
10. October	It's October.
11. November	It's November.
12. December	It's December.
13. cold	It's cold here.
14. warm	It's warm here.
15. hot	It's hot here.
16. rainy	It's rainy here.
17. sunny	It's sunny here.
18. cloudy	It's cloudy here.

Lesson 2. (page 54)
2. Learn New Words
Look at the pictures. Listen to the words.
Then listen and repeat.

1. doctor's appointment	Her doctor's appointment is on May first.
2. computer class	Her computer class is on May third.
3. birthday party	Her birthday party is on May sixth.

4. PTO meeting	Her PTO meeting is on May eighth.
5. job interview	Her job interview is on May ninth.
6. basketball game	Her basketball game is on May eleventh.
7. dentist's appointment	Her dentist's appointment is on May fifteenth.

Lesson 3. (page 56)
1. Learn Ordinal Numbers
Listen to the numbers. Then listen and repeat.

seventeenth	The seventeenth of June is a Sunday.
eighteenth	The eighteenth of June is a Monday.
nineteenth	The nineteenth of June is a Tuesday.
twentieth	The twentieth of June is a Wednesday.
twenty-first	The twenty-first of June is a Thursday.
twenty-second	The twenty-second of June is a Friday.
twenty-third	The twenty-third of June is a Saturday.
twenty-fourth	The twenty-fourth of June is a Sunday.
twenty-fifth	The twenty-fifth of June is a Monday.
twenty-sixth	The twenty-sixth of June is a Tuesday.
twenty-seventh	The twenty-seventh of June is a Wednesday.
twenty-eighth	The twenty-eighth of June is a Thursday.

Lesson 7. (page 64)
1. Listening Review
Listen and choose the word you hear.
Use the Answer Sheet.

1. country	country
2. months	months
3. holidays	holidays
4. family	family
5. dollars	dollars
6. cents	cents
7. state	state
8. cities	cities

Listen and choose the best answer.
Use the Answer Sheet.

9. How many days are in a week?
10. What's the first month of the year?
11. What day is the twenty-first?
12. What day is between Monday and Wednesday?
13. What month is between July and September?
14. When's Thanksgiving in the United States?

Listen and choose the correct appointment card.
Use the Answer Sheet.

15. His appointment is on Wednesday.
16. Her appointment is on Friday.

UNIT FIVE
Lesson 1. (page 68)
1. Learn New Words
Look at the pictures. Listen to the words.
Then listen and repeat.

1. necktie	What is it? It's a necktie.
2. undershirt	What is it? It's an undershirt.
3. briefs	What are they? They're briefs.
4. shoes	What are they? They're shoes.
5. boots	What are they? They're boots.
6. coat	What is it? It's a coat.
7. shirt	What is it? It's a shirt.
8. sweater	What is it? It's a sweater.
9. hat	What is it? It's a hat.
10. T-shirt	What is it? It's a T-shirt.
11. jacket	What is it? It's a jacket.
12. pajamas	What are they? They're pajamas.
13. socks	What are they? They're socks.
14. pants	What are they? They're pants.
15. shorts	What are they? They're shorts.
16. blouse	What is it? It's a blouse.
17. skirt	What is it? It's a skirt.
18. dress	What is it? It's a dress.

Lesson 1. (page 68)
2. Learn New Words
Look at the squares. Listen to the colors.
Then listen and repeat.

1. blue	What color is it? Blue.
2. yellow	What color is it? Yellow.
3. red	What color is it? Red.
4. black	What color is it? Black.
5. brown	What color is it? Brown.
6. green	What color is it? Green.
7. purple	What color is it? Purple.
8. white	What color is it? White.

Lesson 2. (page 70)
1. Learn New Words
Look at the picture. Listen to the words.
Then listen and repeat.
PEOPLE AND PLACES

1. department store	This is Lane's Department Store.
2. fitting room	The fitting room is near the elevator.
3. customer	A customer is near the exit.
4. customer service	There is a woman working at customer service.
5. cashier	The cashier is near the entrance.
6. exit	The exit is across from customer service.
7. entrance	There are people coming in the entrance.

ACTIONS

8. coming into	The man is coming into the store.
9. going into	The woman is going into the elevator.
10. talking	The men are talking about the T-shirt.
11. sleeping	The boy is sleeping near the fitting room.
12. leaving	Marc is leaving the store.
13. running	A cashier is running after Tom.
14. buying	The woman is buying many things.

Lesson 3. (page 72)
1. Learn New Words
Look at the pictures. Listen to the words.
Then listen and repeat.

1. price tag   Where's the price tag?
2. receipt   Where's the receipt?
3. size   What size is it?
4. small   What size is it? It's a small.
5. medium   What size is it? It's a medium.
6. large   What size is it? It's a large.
7. extra large   What size is it? It's an extra large.

Lesson 4. (page 74)
3. Predict
What is the missing word at the end of the story? Share ideas with your classmates. Then listen and compare.
Simon: Here you are, Leo. Your old vest is now a hat.

Lesson 5. (page 76)
1. Learn New Words
Look at the pictures. Listen to the words.
Then listen and repeat.

1. long   The black skirt is long.
2. short   The green skirt is short.
3. too long   The black skirt is too long.
4. too short   The green skirt is too short.
5. tight   The brown pants are tight.
6. loose   The black pants are loose.
7. too tight   The brown pants are too tight.
8. too loose   The black pants are too loose.

Lesson 7. (page 80)
1. Listening Review
Listen and choose the correct answer.
Use the Answer Sheet.

1. What color is his sweater?
2. What's he wearing?
3. Where are the children's clothes?
4. What size is the T-shirt?
5. Is it on sale?
6. What's the price?
7. What's the problem with your shoes?
8. Is it too short?

Lesson 7. (page 80)
2. Dictation
Listen and write the questions you hear.

1. What are you wearing today?
2. What's your favorite color?
3. Do you like baseball caps?

UNIT SIX
Lesson 2. (page 86)
2. Learn New Words
Look at the picture. Listen to the words.
Then listen and repeat.

1. Aisle 1   Where's Aisle 1?
2. restroom   Where's the restroom?

3. ice   Where's the ice?
4. frozen foods   Where are the frozen foods?
5. produce section   Where's the produce section?
6. shopping cart   Where is a shopping cart?
7. mop   Where's the mop?
8. checkout counter   Where's the checkout counter?
9. coupons   Where are the coupons?
10. bakery   Where's the bakery?
11. pushing a cart   Who is pushing a cart?
12. looking at   Who is looking at something?
13. eating   Who is eating something?
14. cleaning the floor   Who is cleaning the floor?
15. standing in line   Who is standing in line?

Lesson 3. (page 88)
1. Learn New Words
Look at the picture. Listen to the words.
Then listen and repeat.

1. a bag of apples   How much is a bag of apples?
2. a carton of milk   How much is a carton of milk?
3. a loaf of bread   How much is a loaf of bread?
4. a package of cheese   How much is a package of cheese?
5. a jar of honey   How much is a jar of honey?
6. a box of sugar   How much is a box of sugar?
7. a can of tomatoes   How much is a can of tomatoes?
8. a bottle of oil   How much is a bottle of oil?
9. expensive   It's expensive.
10. cheap   It's cheap.

Lesson 5. (page 93)
Window on Pronunciation
Intonation in *Yes/No* Questions
Listen to the sentences. Then listen and repeat.

1. A. The apples are on sale.
   B. The apples are on sale?
2. A. Okay?
   B. Okay.
3. A. Milk.
   B. Milk?

Lesson 7. (page 96)
1. Listening Review
Listen and choose the word you hear.
Use the Answer Sheet.

1. I always eat rice for dinner.
2. I sometimes eat cereal in the morning.
3. She usually eats lunch at noon.
4. They never eat in a restaurant on Sunday.

Listen and choose the best answer.
Use the Answer Sheet.

5. Excuse me. Where's the rice?
6. Excuse me. Do you sell ice?
7. How much is a bottle of grape juice?
8. What size bag is it?
9. What's on sale?
10. What can I get for you?

Lesson 7. (page 96)
2. Dictation
Listen and write the missing words.

Attention, shoppers. If you like cereal for breakfast, Corn Crunch is on sale today. It's only three ninety-five for a 12-ounce box. With milk and bananas, your breakfast will be delicious and nutritious. The bananas are in the produce section, and the milk is in the dairy section.

UNIT SEVEN
Lesson 1. (page 100)
1. Learn New Words
Look at the pictures. Listen to the words.
Then listen and repeat.

1. husband	Jack is Mei's husband.
2. wife	Mei is Jack's wife.
3. parents	Jack and Mei are parents.
	They are Ann and Tim's parents.
4. children	Ann and Tim are children.
	They are Jack and Mei's children.
5. mother	Mei is Ann's mother.
6. daughter	Ann is Mei's daughter.
7. father	Jack is Tim's father.
8. son	Tim is Jack's son.
9. sister	Ann is Tim's sister.
10. brother	Tim is Ann's brother.
11. grandmother	Carol is Tim's grandmother.
12. grandson	Tim is Carol's grandson.
13. grandfather	Bob is Ann's grandfather.
14. granddaughter	Ann is Bob's granddaughter.

Lesson 2. (page 102)
1. Learn New Words
Look at the pictures. Listen to the words.
Then listen and repeat.

1. fix things	Do you fix things at home?
2. make the beds	Do you make the beds at home?
3. wash the dishes	Do you wash the dishes at home?
4. take out the trash	Do you take out the trash at home?
5. buy the groceries	Do you buy the groceries?
6. pay the bills	Do you pay the bills at home?
7. clean the house	Do you clean the house?
8. do the laundry	Do you do the laundry at home?
9. cook dinner	Do you cook dinner at home?

Lesson 3. (page 104)
2. Learn New Words
Look at the picture. Listen to the words.
Then listen and repeat.

1. read the newspaper	Do you read the newspaper?
2. play an instrument	Do you play an instrument?
3. dance	Do you dance?
4. play cards	Do you play cards?
5. take pictures	Do you take pictures?
6. listen to music	Do you listen to music?
7. play soccer	Do you play soccer?
8. tell stories	Do you tell stories?

Lesson 6. (page 110)
1. Learn New Words
Look at the pictures below. Listen to the words.
Then listen and repeat.

1. rent	How much do you spend on rent?
2. transportation	How much do you spend on transportation?
3. groceries	How much do you spend on groceries?
4. education	How much do you spend on education?
5. child care	How much do you spend on child care?
6. utilities	How much do you spend on utilities?
7. clothing	How much do you spend on clothing?
8. savings	How much do you save?
9. gifts	How much do you give away?

Lesson 6. (page 110)
2. Give Opinions
Listen to a conversation with Mr. Garcia.
Check your guesses.

Interviewer:	How much do you spend on rent?
Mr. Garcia:	The rent on our apartment is $1,000 a month.
Interviewer:	And transportation. How much do you spend on transportation?
Mr. Garcia:	Well, I take the bus to work, but we also have a car. We spend about $900 a year for car and bus expenses.
Interviewer:	What about groceries?
Mr. Garcia:	We usually spend about $60 a week or $240 a month on food.
Interviewer:	Do you spend money on education?
Mr. Garcia:	Yes. My wife is taking a computer course, and my son needs school supplies and books. I think we spend about $800 a year on education.
Interviewer:	Do you spend any money on child care?
Mr. Garcia:	Yes, for my daughter. She goes to day care three days a week. That costs $300 a month.
Interviewer:	What about utilities?
Mr. Garcia:	Do you mean heat and electricity?
Interviewer:	Yes.
Mr. Garcia:	Well, we spend about $75 a month for utilities.
Interviewer:	And clothing? Is that a big expense?
Mr. Garcia:	I don't know. My wife says we spend about $1,500 a year on clothes.
Interviewer:	Can you save any money?
Mr. Garcia:	It's difficult with two children, but we try to save $2,000 every year.
Interviewer:	That's great. What about gifts? Do you give money away?
Mr. Garcia:	Yes, we try to give $200 a year to a local charity.

Lesson 7. (page 112)
1. Listening Review
Look at the family tree. Listen and choose the best answer. Use the Answer Sheet.

1. What's Carol's husband's name?
2. Who's Mei?
3. Who's Ann?
4. Who's Tim's grandmother?

Listen and choose the best answer. Use the Answer Sheet.

5. Do you live with your parents?
6. What's your brother's name?
7. Does John have children?
8. Who does the dishes in your family?
9. Where do your parents live?
10. What does she do at home?
11. Do you play an instrument?
12. How often do her children cook dinner?

UNIT EIGHT
Lesson 2. (page 118)
2. Learn New Words
Look at the picture. Listen to the words. Then listen and repeat.

1. headache   Tina has a headache.
2. earache   Martin's son has an earache.
3. fever   Louis has a fever.
4. runny nose   Ken has a runny nose.
5. cough   Rose's daughter has a cough.
6. sore throat   Donna has a sore throat.
7. backache   Erik has a backache.
8. stomachache   Tom has a stomachache.

Lesson 3. (page 120)
1. Learn New Words
Look at the pictures. Listen to the words. Then listen and repeat.

1. A: Drink liquids. B: Drink what? A: Liquids.
2. A: Eat soft foods. B: Eat what? A: Soft foods.
3. A: Take cough medicine. B: Take what? A: Cough medicine.
4. A: Take aspirin. B: Take what? A: Aspirin.
5. A: Use ear drops. B: Use what? A: Ear drops.
6. A: Rest. B: Rest? A: Rest.
7. A: Put heat on it. B: Put what on it? A: Heat.
8. A: Put ice on it. B: Put what on it? A: Ice.
9. A: Bandage it. B: Do what to it? A: Bandage it.
10. A: Keep it dry. B: Keep it what? A: Dry.

Lesson 5. (page 124)
1. Learn New Words
Look at the pictures below. Listen to the words. Then listen and repeat.

1. He is choking. What's the matter? He's choking.
2. He is bleeding. What's the matter? He's bleeding.
3. She is having a heart attack. What's the matter? She's having a heart attack.
4. She isn't breathing. What's the matter? She isn't breathing.

Lesson 5. (page 125)
Window on Pronunciation
Linking Vowel to Vowel with a *Y* or *W* Sound
Listen and complete the conversations.

1.
A: This is 911.
B: My mother is hurt. She's choking.
A: Where are you?
B: I'm at 414 Pine Street.

2.
A: Where are you?
B: We're at home.
A: How's Paul?
B: He's resting.

Lesson 6. (page 126)
1. Learn New Words
Look at the pictures. Listen to the words. Then listen and repeat.

1. Main Entrance   Where's the main entrance?
2. Emergency Entrance   Where's the emergency entrance?
3. Lobby   Where's the lobby?
4. Visitors' Lounge   Where's the visitors' lounge?

Lesson 7. (page 128)
1. Listening Review
Listen to the conversations. Choose the problem you hear. Use the Answer Sheet.

1.
A: What's the matter?
B: My wrist hurts.
A: Can you move it?
B: Yes, a little.

2.
A: What's the matter with Thomas?
B: He has a really bad headache.
A: That's too bad.

3.
A: Can I help you?
B: Yes, I have an appointment with Dr. Jones.
A: What are you here for, Mr. Munro?
B: It's my ear. I have an earache.

4.
A: Hi, I'm Dr. Coffin.
B: Hi, Dr. Coffin. I'm John Fernandez.
A: Nice to meet you. So what's the problem?
B: Oh, I have a sore shoulder.

Listen and choose the best answer. Use the Answer Sheet.

5. What should I do for my backache?
6. What should you do for a stomachache?
7. What number should you call for an ambulance?
8. Should you call 911 for a sore toe?

UNIT NINE
Lesson 1. (page 132)
1. Learn New Words
Look at the pictures. Listen to the words.
Then listen and repeat.

1. sofa — Where's the sofa?
2. bookcase — Where's the bookcase?
3. lamp — Where's the lamp?
4. smoke alarm — Where's the smoke alarm?
5. carpet — Where's the carpet?
6. mirror — Where's the mirror?
7. sink — Where's the sink?
8. shower — Where's the shower?
9. toilet — Where's the toilet?
10. bathtub — Where's the bathtub?
11. drawer — Where's the drawer?
12. cabinet — Where's the cabinet?
13. closet — Where's the closet?
14. refrigerator — Where's the refrigerator?
15. stove — Where's the stove?
16. dresser — Where's the dresser?
17. bed — Where's the bed?

Lesson 2. (page 134)
1. Learn New Words
Look at the pictures. Listen to the words.
Then listen and repeat.

1. pool — Does your house have a pool?
2. patio — Does your house have a patio?
3. front yard — Does your house have a front yard?
4. carport — Does your house have a carport?
5. driveway — Does your house have a driveway?
6. garage — Does your house have a garage?
7. porch — Does your house have a porch?
8. backyard — Does your house have a backyard?
9. garden — Does your house have a garden?

Lesson 3. (page 136)
1. Learn New Words
Look at the pictures. Listen to the words.
Then listen and repeat.

1. fell down the stairs
   A: What happened to Joe?
   B: He fell down the stairs.
2. fell off a ladder
   A: What happened to Sylvia?
   B: She fell off a ladder.
3. fell off a chair
   A: What happened to Carol?
   B: She fell off a chair.
4. slipped in the shower
   A: What happened to Mike?
   B: He slipped in the shower.
5. cut his hand with a knife
   A: What happened to Nick?
   B: He cut his hand with a knife.
6. tripped on the carpet
   A: What happened to Donna?
   B: She tripped on the carpet.

Lesson 4. (page 138)
1. Learn New Words
Look at the pictures. Listen to the words.
Then listen and repeat.

1. apartment — Do you live in an apartment?
2. condo — Do you live in a condo?
3. mobile home — Do you live in a mobile home?

Lesson 4. (page 138)
2. Write
Read and listen to the classified ads.
Find and write the abbreviations for these words.

a. House for rent. Three bedrooms, two bathrooms. Near schools. Patio and pool. $1350 per month. Call Eileen at 555-4000.
b. For rent. Mobile home. One bedroom, one bathroom. Near public pool. $795 per month. Call Joe, 555-1928.
c. House for sale. Three bedrooms, two bathrooms, big kitchen, two fireplaces, patio, garage. $210,000. Call Marlene, 555-1200, ext. 15.
d. For rent, two bedroom, two bathroom apartment. Pool and patio. $950. Call John, 555-4583.
e. For sale. Two bedroom, one-and-a-half bathroom condo. Near stores. $175,000. Call Smith Realty, 555-6767.
f. Apartment for rent. One bedroom, one bathroom. $825 per month. Call 555-9904.
g. Condo for rent. Two bedrooms, one bathroom, garage, near schools, $1100 per month. Call Bev, 555-4954.
h. Mobile home for rent. Two bedroom, one bathroom, patio, no pets, $875 per month. Call 555-9948.

Lesson 6. (page 142)
1. Learn New Words
Look at the bills below. Listen to the words.
Then listen and repeat.

1. account number — The account number is 6464560483-0.
2. amount due — The amount due is $133.19.
3. amount enclosed — The amount enclosed is $133.19.
4. new charges — The amount of new charges is $56.29.

Lesson 7. (page 144)
1. Listening Review
Listen to the conversations. Choose the correct picture.
Use the Answer Sheet.

1. A: Where's my blue sweater?
   B: It's in your dresser.
   A: Oh, thanks.
2. A: Where's Joe?
   B: He's in the kitchen
   A: What's he doing there?
   B: He's cleaning the stove.
3. A: I'm calling about the apartment for rent.
   B: Yes. What do you want to know?
   A: Can you tell me, does it have a patio?
   B: Yes, it does. It has a beautiful patio.
4. A: What happened to your brother?
   B: He fell off a ladder.
   A: That's too bad. Is he okay now?
   B: Yes, he's fine.

Listen and choose the best answer.
Use the Answer Sheet.

5. Where's the smoke alarm?
6. Does the apartment have a shower?
7. Do you live in an apartment?
8. How many bedrooms does it have?

UNIT TEN
Lesson 1. (page 148)
1. Learn New Words
Look at the pictures. Listen to the words.
Then listen and repeat.

1. chef	A chef cooks food.
2. office manager	An office manager uses a computer.
3. plumber	A plumber repairs sinks and toilets.
4. stylist	A stylist cuts hair.
5. child care worker	A child care worker takes care of children.
6. mechanic	A mechanic fixes cars.
7. mover	A mover lifts heavy things.
8. construction worker	A construction worker builds things.
9. truck driver	A truck driver drives a truck.
10. landscaper	A landscaper takes care of plants.

Lesson 3. (page 152)
2. Listen and Take Notes
Listen to Rosa's job interview. Write the missing information.

Interviewer:	So, Rosa, tell me about yourself.
Interviewee:	Well, I'm really interested in retail. Right now I'm the store manager at Lane's. I got the job in 2000.
Interviewer:	That's very interesting. Do you like your job?
Interviewee:	Yes, very much. I'm really sad Lane's is closing soon.
Interviewer:	Yes, that is too bad. And what did you do before that?
Interviewee:	Well, I was a salesclerk at Lane's for almost two years, from 1998 to 2000. Then I got promoted to store manager.
Interviewer:	Yes, I see.
Interviewee:	And before that, I worked as a salesclerk at a store called The Elephant's Trunk.
Interviewer:	When was that?
Interviewee:	I worked there from 1996 to 1998. I learned a lot there.

Lesson 7. (page 160)
1. Listening Review
Listen and choose the correct answer.
Use the Answer Sheet.

1. What do stylists do?
2. Can he lift heavy things?
3. Did she work last week?
4. Is it a part-time job?
5. Why did you leave your last job?
6. Why should I hire you?
7. Sam worked 10 hours last week. He earns $20 an hour. How much did he earn last week?
8. Mei worked 40 hours last week. She earns $20 an hour. How much did she earn last week?

Lesson 7. (page 160)
2. Dictation
Listen and write the questions you hear.

1. Did you work last year?
2. Can you drive a car?
3. Do you have a job now?

Numbers in parentheses indicate unit numbers.

accident (9)
account number (9)
across from (2)
address (1)
after (3)
afternoon (3)
aisle (6)
always (6)
A.M. (3)
ambulance (2)
amount (3)
amount due (9)
amount enclosed (9)
ankle (8)
apartment (9)
apple (6)
appointment (4)
April (4)
area code (1)
arm (8)
ask (1)
ask questions (10)
aspirin (8)
ATM (2)
audiobook (2)
August (4)
aunt (7)
back (8)
backache (8)
backyard (9)
bag (6)
bakery (6)
banana (6)
bandage (8)
bank (2)
basketball game (4)
bathroom (9)
bathtub (9)
be (1)
be late (10)
bean (6)
bed (9)
bedroom (9)
before (3)
benefits (10)
between (2)
big (5)
birthday party (4)
birthplace (1)
black (5)
bleed (8)
blouse (5)
blue (5)
board (1)
book (1)
bookcase (9)
bookmobile (2)
boot (5)
bottle (6)
box (6)
bread (6)
breathe (8)
briefs (5)

brother (7)
brown (5)
budget (7)
build (10)
bus (2)
bus driver (1)
bus stop (2)
butter (6)
buy (5)
cabinet (9)
calendar (1)
can (6)
cap (5)
capital (2)
car (2)
carefully (10)
carpet (9)
carport (9)
carrot (6)
carton (6)
cashier (1)
cents (3)
cereal (6)
chair (1)
cheap (6)
check (3)
check number (3)
checkout counter (6)
checkout desk (2)
cheese (6)
chef (10)
chest (8)
chew gum (10)
chicken (6)
child care (7)
child care worker (10)
children (7)
children's book (2)
choke (8)
circle (1)
city (1)
clean (6)
clock (1)
close (1)
closed (3)
closet (9)
clothing (7)
cloudy (4)
coat (5)
cold (4)
coming into (5)
comma (1)
community center (2)
computer (1)
condo (9)
construction worker (10)
cook (10)
cook dinner (7)
cooked (6)
cough (8)
cough medicine (8)
country (1)
coupon (6)

crosswalk (2)
cup (6)
customer (5)
customer service (5)
cut (5)
dairy (6)
dance (7)
daughter (7)
day (3)
December (4)
delicious (6)
dentist (1)
department store (5)
desk (1)
dime (3)
dining room (9)
dish (7)
divided by (5)
divorced (1)
doctor (1)
dollar (3)
door (1)
do the laundry (7)
drawer (9)
dress (5/noun)
dress (10/verb)
dresser (9)
drink (8)
drive (10)
driveway (9)
drugstore (2)
dry (8)
ear (8)
earache (8)
ear drops (8)
east (2)
eat (6)
education (7)
egg (6)
eight (1)
eighteen (3)
eighteenth (4)
eighth (4)
eighty (3)
elbow (8)
eleven (1)
eleventh (4)
emergency entrance (8)
enter (2)
entrance (5)
equals (2)
evening (3)
exit (5)
expense (7)
expensive (6)
extra large (5)
eye (8)
fall (9)
father (7)
February (4)
feet (8)
female (1)
fever (8)

fifteen (3)
fifteenth (4)
fifth (4)
fifty (3)
fine (1)
finger (8)
fire station (2)
first (4)
fish (6)
fitting room (5)
five (1)
fix (7)
flammable (8)
floor (1)
food (6)
foot (8)
forty (3)
four (1)
fourteen (3)
fourteenth (4)
fourth (4)
Friday (3)
front yard (9)
frozen foods (6)
fruit (6)
gallon (8)
garage (9)
garden (9)
gas station (2)
gender (1)
gift (7)
go to (1)
going into (5)
grain (6)
granddaughter (7)
grandfather (7)
grandmother (7)
grandson (7)
grape (6)
green (5)
grocery (7)
half-dollar (3)
hand (8)
hat (5)
have (6)
head (8)
headache (8)
heart attack (8)
heat (8)
heavy (10)
hole (5)
honey (6)
hospital (2)
hot (4)
hours (3)
husband (7)
ice (6)
indoor (10)
in back of (2)
in front of (2)
internally (8)
jacket (5)
January (4)

Vocabulary List

jar (6)
job interview (4)
juice (6)
July (4)
June (4)
kitchen (9)
knee (8)
knife (9)
ladder (9)
lamp (9)
landscaper (10)
large (5)
late (10)
laundromat (2)
leave (5)
left (2)
leg (8)
less than (2)
lettuce (6)
librarian (2)
library (2)
library card (2)
lift (10)
like (6)
liquid (8)
listen (1)
listen carefully (10)
listen to music (7)
living room (9)
loaf (6)
lobby (8)
long (5)
look at (6)
look for (5)
loose (5)
machinist (1)
magazine (2)
mailbox (2)
main entrance (8)
make (10)
make the bed (7)
male (1)
map (1)
March (4)
marital status (1)
married (1)
May (4)
meat (6)
mechanic (10)
medium (5)
men (5)
middle name (1)
midnight (3)
milk (6)
minus (2)
minute (3)
mirror (9)
mobile home (9)
Monday (3)
month (4)
mop (6)
more than (2)
morning (3)

mother (7)
mouth (8)
mover (10)
movie theater (2)
Mr. (1)
Mrs. (1)
Ms. (1)
near (2)
neatly (10)
neck (8)
necktie (5)
never (6)
new charges (9)
newspaper (7)
next to (2)
nickel (3)
night (3)
nine (1)
nineteen (3)
nineteenth (4)
ninety (3)
ninth (4)
noodles (6)
noon (3)
north (2)
nose (8)
notebook (1)
November (4)
nurse (1)
nut (6)
occupation (1)
o'clock (3)
October (4)
office manager (10)
oil (6)
on sale (6)
on the corner of (2)
one (1)
one way (2)
onion (6)
open (1/verb)
open (3/adj.)
orange (6)
ounce (6)
outdoor (10)
out of reach (8)
package (6)
pajamas (5)
pants (5)
parent (7)
park (2)
parking lot (2)
partner (1)
patio (9)
pay phone (2)
pay the bills (7)
peanut (6)
pen (1)
pencil (1)
penny (3)
people (1)
period (1)
personal check (3)

pharmacist (1)
piece of paper (1)
pint (8)
play an instrument
   (7)
play cards (7)
play soccer (7)
plumber (10)
plus (2)
P.M. (3)
poison (8)
police officer (1)
police station (2)
pool (9)
porch (9)
post office (2)
pound (6)
practice (1)
pregnant (8)
price (5)
price tag (5)
produce section (6)
PTO meeting (4)
purple (5)
push a cart (6)
quart (8)
quarter (3)
question mark (1)
question (10)
rainy (4)
raise (1)
raw (6)
read (1)
receipt (5)
red (5)
refrigerator (9)
reliable (10)
rent (7)
repair (10)
repeat (1)
rest (8)
restaurant (2)
restroom (6)
rice (6)
right (2)
run (5)
runny nose (8)
sale (9)
salesclerk (1)
Saturday (3)
savings (7)
say (1)
school (2)
scissors (5)
second (4)
September (4)
serving (6)
seven (1)
seventeen (3)
seventeenth (4)
seventh (4)
seventy (3)
shake hands (10)

shirt (5)
shoe (5)
shopping cart (6)
short (5)
shorts (5)
shoulder (8)
shower (9)
shrimp (6)
sidewalk (2)
signature (3)
single (1)
sink (9)
sister (7)
sit down (1)
six (1)
sixteen (3)
sixteenth (4)
sixth (4)
sixty (3)
size (5)
skirt (5)
slice (6)
sleep (5)
slip (9)
small (5)
smoke alarm (9)
smoking (3)
sock (5)
sofa (9)
soft food (8)
sometimes (6)
son (7)
sore (8)
south (2)
stairs (9)
stand in line (6)
stand up (1)
state (1)
stomach (8)
stomachache (8)
stop (2)
stoplight (2)
stove (9)
street (1)
student (1)
stylist (10)
sugar (6)
Sunday (3)
sunny (4)
supermarket (2)
sweater (5)
table (1)
tailor (5)
take care of (10)
take out (1)
take pictures (7)
talk to (5)
taxi (2)
teacher (1)
telephone number
   (1)
tell stories (7)
ten (1)

tenth (4)
terrible (6)
third (4)
thirteen (3)
thirteenth (4)
thirtieth (4)
thirty (3)
thirty-five (3)
thirty-one (3)
three (1)
throat (8)
Thursday (3)
tight (5)
times (5)
toe (8)
toilet (9)
tomato (6)
too (5)
transportation (7)
trash (7)
trip (9)
truck (2)
truck driver (10)
T-shirt (5)
Tuesday (3)
turn (2)
twelfth (4)
twelve (3)
twentieth (4)
twenty (3)
twenty-one (3)
two (1)
uncle (7)
undershirt (5)
usually (6)
utilities (7)
vegetable (6)
video (2)
visitor's lounge (8)
wall (1)
warm (4)
wash (7)
weather (4)
wear (5)
Wednesday (3)
week (3)
west (2)
white (5)
wife (7)
window (1)
women (5)
wrist (8)
write (1)
yellow (5)
yogurt (6)
zero (1)
zip code (1)

Conversations, 114
Dates, 55, 56-57
Description, 76, 106, 134, 148
Dictation, 32, 80, 96, 160
Graphs, charts, and maps, 3, 4, 8, 15, 17, 35, 42, 47, 49, 52, 56, 58–59, 63, 68, 84, 85, 88, 94–95, 97, 100, 106, 111, 113, 116, 131, 134, 150, 152
Instructions, 8, 99
Lists, 20, 52, 72, 84, 90, 111, 122, 163
Money, 40-41
Name tags, 3
Numbers, 42
Opinions, 152
Paragraphs, 102, 131 (expository)
Personal information, 3, 17, 18–19
Questions, 50–51, 83, 101, 104, 114–115
Questions, answering, 50, 62, 111
Receipts, 72
Recipes, 99
Statements, 4, 18–19, 38, 46, 52, 74, 76, 79, 82, 86, 95, 102, 104, 106, 114, 118, 126, 132, 134, 146, 148, 150, 152–153, 154
Stories, 34-35, 67, 152, 162
Time, 36-38, 45
Vocabulary, 6, 10, 15, 30, 36-37, 38, 40–41, 52–53, 66, 68, 100, 102–103, 132

APPLICATION

Community, 30–31, 46–47, 126–127
Family, 62–63, 94–95, 110–111, 142–143
Work, 14–15, 78–79, 158–159

LEARNER LOGS

17, 33, 49, 65, 81, 97, 113, 129, 145, 161

LIFE SKILLS

Consumer Education

Advertisements, 90–91, 96, 138–139
Checks, 42-43
Clothing items, 68–69, 72–73, 74–75, 76–77, 78–79, 80–81
Counting money, 40–41
Food items, 84–89, 92–97
Hours of operation, 46
Household/housing, 110–111, 132–-145
Making transactions, 77, 81, 92–93
Prices, 41, 47, 72–73, 80–81, 90–91, 92–93, 96–97
Product labels, 122–123
Receipts, 72–73, 90
Sales, 72–73, 93

Shopping lists, 90
Sizes, 72–73
Stores, 20–21, 70–71
Utility companies, 142

Environment and World

Building maps, 126–127
City maps, 22–25, 32–33
United States map, 26–27
Weather, 52–53, 65
World map, 4-5

Family and Parenting

Family members, 100–113
Family responsibilities, 102–103
Household/housing, 110–111, 132–145
Recipes, 98–99

Government and Community

Agencies, 20
Leisure activities, 104–105
Library, 22, 30–31
Medical services, 124–125, 126–127
Places in the community, 20–25, 32–33
Post Office, 20, 22–23, 24–25
Public services, 20, 22, 24–25
Signs, 24–25, 38–39, 46-47, 70–71

Group Work

3, 4, 88, 120, 148

Resources

Community places, 20–25, 32–33
Library, 22, 30–31
Post Office, 20, 22–23, 24–25
Public services, 20, 22, 24–25

Health and Nutrition

Accidents, 136–137
Body part identification, 116–117
Foods and food groups, 84–85, 88–89, 94–99
Health care vocabulary, 118–129
Hospital, 126–127
Medical advice, 120, 128–129
Medicine labels and use, 122–123
Symptoms and illnesses, 116–117, 118–119, 120–121, 124–125, 128–129

Interpersonal Communication

Introductions, greetings, and farewells, 2–5, 12–13
Personal information, 4–5, 10–11, 17, 50
Understanding instructions, 8–9, 98–99

Learning to Learn

Problem solving skills, 74–75
Thinking skills, 74–75, 90, 122–123

Pair Work

2–3, 6, 8–9, 10, 12–13, 14, 22–23, 24, 28--29, 36–37, 38, 40–41, 43, 44, 51, 52--53, 56, 60–61, 68, 70, 72, 76–77, 78, 83, 84, 88, 92–93, 97, 100–101, 102, 104, 106, 108–109, 110–111, 113, 114, 116, 118, 120, 124–125, 126, 129, 134, 136, 140–141, 145, 147, 150, 156-157, 159, 161

Safety and Security

Emergency procedures, 124–125, 128
Product labels, 122–123
Warning labels and symbols, 122–123

Telephone Communication

Answering, 108
Making a call, 108
Making appointments, 60–61, 65
Messages, taking and leaving, 109
Obtaining information, 44–45, 140–141
911 use, 124–125

Time and Money

Appointments, 60–61, 64–65
Bills, 142–143
Budgets, 110–111, 113
Days of the week, 38–39
Calendar, 54–55, 62–63
Checks, 42–43, 142–143
Clock time, 36–39, 48–49
Coins and currency, 40–41
Date format, 56–57
Months, 52–53, 64–65
Numbers, cardinal and ordinal, 9, 27, 36, 54–57, 64, 70
Receipts, 72–73

Transportation and Travel

Geographical directions and locations, 26–27
Traffic signs, 24–25
Types, 24–25

TOPICS

Activities, 102–105
Body Parts, 116–117
Classroom, 6–7, 8–9, 16
Clothing, 68–69, 72–81
Colors, 68–69
Community, 22–25, 28–33

Map of the United States

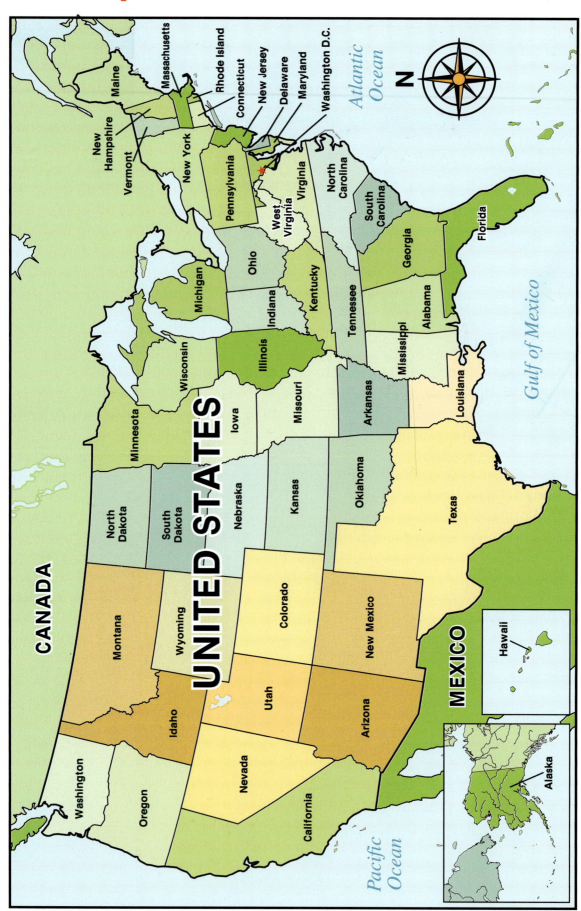